The
TIES
That
BIND
… *and Bind*

… *and Bind*

The Ties That Bind...

and Bind... and Bind

A Survival Guide to In-Law Relationships

SYLVIA BIGELSEN

ELEMENT

Boston, Massachusetts • Shaftesbury, Dorset
Melbourne, Victoria

Text © Sylvia Bigelsen 1999
© Element Books, Inc. 1999

Published in the USA in 1999 by
Element Books, Inc.
160 North Washington Street
Boston, MA 02114

Published in Great Britain in 1999 by
Element Books Limited
Shaftesbury, Dorset SP7 8BP

Published in Australia in 1999 by
Element Books Limited for
Penguin Australia Limited
487 Maroondah Highway, Ringwood, Victoria 3134

Library of Congress Cataloging-in-Publication Data

Bigelsen, Sylvia.
    The ties that bind and bind and bind : a survival guide to
in-law relationships / Sylvia Bigelsen.
        p.   cm.
    Includes bibliographical references and index.
    ISBN 1-86204-487-2 (pbk. : alk. paper)
    1. Parents-in-law — United States. 2. Interpersonal
relations — United States..
    I. Title.
    HQ759.8.B54 1999
    646.7'8—dc21   99-019528
                                                             CIP

Printed and bound in the United States by Courier

ACKNOWLEDGMENTS

This book is the product of years of personal and professional experience, and over that time I have listened to friends, family members, and clients as they shared their stories and dilemmas. As we talked over and worked through their problems—and sometimes mine—I learned so much about the way the in-law connection affects individuals over a lifetime. I am deeply grateful to these women and men who willingly shared their disappointments and frustrations and also their attempts to find solutions.

Virginia McCullough, a book author in her own right, has been my greatest source of help and encouragement. My work was made easier because of her editorial skills. But even more than the practical help, I appreciate her enthusiasm for this book and her constant support and friendship.

I also thank Fred, my dear husband of so many years. He recognized that the in-law relationships in our lives provided the "hands on" experience that gave me the insight necessary to help others.

INTRODUCTION

*W*hen the in-law relationship is going well,
it can be a joy, perhaps even a delightful
—and unexpected—addition to a satisfying marriage. But
when it's going poorly, it can cause untold heartbreak and
pain. The term "in-law relationship" here refers to the whole
spectrum of these special bonds, from parents-in-law to
brothers/sisters-in-law, and nowadays, even the in-law grandparents many people acquire when they marry. It also
includes the array of in-laws one acquires in a second (or
third) marriage, even while an ongoing relationship continues with the original in-law group.

As unique as your problems may seem, remember that
from the beginning of human life on our planet, structures
and institutions have created new families and established
ways to form bonds with the relatives that come with the
marriage "package." And let's not forget that the family,
with all its variations, was created to regulate procreation.
While this may sound unromantic, perpetuating our species
in a proscribed and acceptable way is the reason for this
institution. We have a saying in our culture: "You can choose
your friends, but you can't choose your relatives." I can

imagine cave people clans and tribes sitting around the camp-fire saying the same thing.

That said, we find ourselves in the midst of still another evolutionary change in the way we structure families. In our culture and many others, men and women have one partner at a time and the ideal is that the mate one chooses is the same mate with whom one will grow old. As we all know, glitches exist in our system, and a high divorce rate or the death of a spouse can break a bond that was intended to be lifelong.

In some cultures, a man or woman marries and becomes identified with either the bride or groom's family, even to the point of being required to live in an extended family environment. In our culture, however, we generally expect the couple to set up their own family unit and live away from either set of parents. In our culture a newly married couple rarely lives with either spouse's parents or grand-parents. Theoretically, our arrangement means that the new family is less tied to either family of origin, and therefore, the problems should be fewer. After all, the newly married couple are free to make their own rules, create their own rituals, and raise children their own way.

I can tell you from long experience that as good as the theory may sound, what actually occurs in many homes, day in and day out throughout Western societies, often brings frustrations, irritations, and minor squabbles, at best, and rage, heartbreak, and broken dreams, at worst. While we don't have reliable statistics to prove my theory, I'm convinced that in-law problems contribute to our high divorce rate and most certainly play a role in driving many couples into family therapy. Even when in-law issues aren't the primary reason for a couple to seek therapy, as time goes on, problems in these relationships usually come up.

Mind you, I'm not necessarily blaming a demanding

father-in-law or a catty sister-in-law for a couple's problems. But unfortunately, when it comes to harmonious agreements about relationships with in-laws, many married people are not able to set guidelines, create their own rules, and reach compromises between themselves as a couple.

Imagine a young groom who expects to spend every holiday with his parents. He might make this assumption because his wife's family is more laid back, so to speak, about their religious traditions. So, the first Easter or Passover rolls around, and his wife says, "We're expected at my parents' house Sunday at four o'clock." "What?" the groom exclaims. "My parents are expecting us at noon. You'll just have to explain to your parents that we can't come."

Depending on how the couple handle this situation, things could get ugly. One partner ends up resentful; the other partner doesn't understand why. My question to such a couple is, "Did you discuss these issues before you were married? What were your expectations?"

As often as not, each partner looks surprised by my questions. Talk about this? "I just assumed . . ." or "I thought it was understood . . ." or "This is the way my family does things" are typical responses. And so it goes, on and on: misunderstandings, arguments, and building resentments.

In some cases, one set of in-laws truly dominates, or an in-law parent is openly nasty. On more than one occasion I've asked individual clients a variation of the following question: "And what did you say when your mother criticized your wife's clothing (or cooking or child-rearing methods)?"

As often as not, the man will just shake his head and say, "Well, nothing really. I guess I thought it would blow over. It didn't seem very important."

Or I've said to a wife: "What did you say to your mother when she was nasty to your husband's sister?"

"I didn't say anything—his sister is really stupid. My mother was right about her—what's to say? *He knows she's an idiot.*"

In the first case, the mother-in-law in question had criticized her daughter-in-law for fifteen years. In the second case, the couple was married all of six months when they came to see me for counseling. They couldn't understand why their young marriage was nearly in shambles already.

Throughout my career as a family therapist, I've heard just about every kind of in-law story you can imagine. I've learned about fathers who won't let go of their daughters and continue to indulge their every desire for expensive vacations and luxury homes. Other stories center around mothers-in-law who rearrange furniture in their sons' houses, claiming that their daughters-in-law have bad taste. Also discussed are the daughters who spend several evenings a week talking with their mothers on the phone and don't see why their husbands find this odd. I've heard about husbands who don't understand why their wives won't pick up after them and balk at doing all the cooking and laundry after they come home from work. After all, good old mom took care of him, why can't his wife?

Then, as married life moves through its natural stages, couples begin arguing about one set of parents who won't, just won't, stop feeding the two-year-old junk food. One couple I worked with were vegetarians, but the grandparents (in this case, the husband's parents) insisted on feeding their grandkids fast-food burgers. The husband, a staunch vegetarian himself, refused to take a stand with his parents, leaving his wife to wonder what kind of wimp she'd married. In this case, the parents ended up divorcing, and the former daughter-in-law was driven to keeping her former in-laws away from her children. Broken relationships—over a hamburger. Seems incredible, but it happens every day.

If you are like most people, you have probably formed your own opinion about the great hamburger conspiracy. On one hand, you could be thinking: What a trivial issue. What harm can an occasional hamburger do? That daughter-in-law really overreacted. Or perhaps you take the other view: Who do those grandparents think they are? They have a lot of nerve going against the parents. Parents have a right to decide what their children eat. What kind of father is that husband anyway?

As we move along through the life cycle of the in-law relationship, we bump up against one potentially sticky problem after another, right down to who takes care of the aging parents. When couples reach middle age, they may still be educating their own children and planning for retirement. Suddenly—or not so suddenly—they are faced with the dilemma of helping out their parents.

The assumptions of the past, which usually dictated that this kind of caregiving was the wife's job, no longer work. One couple came to my office when they had reached an impasse about having an in-law, who could no longer live alone, move in with them. The husband assumed that his wife would quit her job—after all, she made less money—and stay home. But this woman loved her work and wouldn't hear of it. The situation was complicated by the fact that the wife had been silently resentful of her mother-in-law's constant needling for almost thirty years. "Why hadn't she spoken up?" the husband asked. Well, early in the marriage she had attempted to talk with her husband about the problems that he apparently could not or would not see. Since he never listened to her when she talked about the problem, she eventually gave up. So, decades later, here they are, in a therapist's office, where he is forced to listen to her bitterness or he'll end up taking care of his mother alone.

Does it have to be this way? Is there a better way? After listening to these problems for many, many years I can say yes, a solution to these problems exists, and it doesn't involve changing the in-laws. I believe that the root of the difficulty comes from the inability of the couple to fully make the psychological break from their families of origin and create an independent unit, with its own set of agreements and compromises. Can anyone do this perfectly? Probably not. But most of us can do better.

I don't imply here that all in-law relationships are fraught with pain and anger. Many in-law relationships are characterized by mutual respect, honesty, and in some cases, genuine love; irritations tend to be minor, and when bigger problems come up, solutions that everyone can live with are possible. These positive in-law relationships do not just happen, however, although a degree of luck sometimes plays a role. Harmonious relationships usually result from a strong bond between a couple that is able to resist the demand for divided loyalties. Sometimes harmony is possible because the in-laws encourage the couple to be independent, and they stay out of their children's marriages. Not all in-laws interfere.

As you read through this book, you will be introduced to dozens of different situations and examples of in-law relationships that were, at least in part, contributing to troubled marriages. Sometimes the parents' marriage is adversely affected by the in-law children. These parents may disagree about the best way to handle their relationships with grown children and their spouses. I've worked with single people who have difficulty with their siblings' spouses, and I've worked with married couples who are immersed in a tug-of-war over how to handle a single brother- or sister-in-law. The possible combinations of players in these dramas, which are too frequently part of family life, have no end.

You may be embroiled in a serious in-law problem right now. Perhaps you are newly married and you see difficulties on the horizon, disagreements you hadn't anticipated. Or perhaps you are several years into a marriage, and problems were brewing all along. An incident forced them to the surface, and both you and your spouse are confused and angry and probably hurt besides. I would like to think that many of you are planning to marry and you want to *prevent* difficulties before they start. But no matter where you are in the life cycle of the in-law relationship, whether you are in-law parents and siblings or you are the newly formed family, the information presented here can help you to:

* look realistically at the origin of relationship difficulties,

* anticipate potential problems and work on solutions before the trouble begins,

* understand the way in which your family of origin influences your assumptions and expectations of marriage and family,

* work toward and expect harmonious solutions to problems,

* recognize when compromise is not possible and make the best decision you can to work around the problem,

* realize that the source of solutions resides with you —you can't change others, you can change only yourself.

We are dealing with a rapidly changing relationship landscape. Every assumption made about family structures has been challenged, from who plans and pays for the wedding to who (if anyone) stays home with the children, to who should remember birthdays and buy the gifts for various family members.

Today's families may resemble a mini-United Nations in their ethnic, racial, and religious diversity. When everybody in a family welcomes diversity, it presents few problems and can offer rich and rewarding experiences. But let prejudice and rigid attitudes prevail, and anger and heartbreak become inevitable.

My hope is that this book will expand your horizons and help you see the possibilities that exist to create a new set of assumptions and attitudes. I hope that a new way of looking at the complexity of family relationships will lead to deeper understanding of yourself, your marriage, and all the other family members that are part of the ties that bind.

Remember that you have a choice about how you behave toward new family members. You can consciously decide to treat in-law parents or in-law children with courtesy and respect. You can make a decision about the way in which you will handle problems as they arise. You do not have to be a helpless victim, nor must you repeat family patterns that hurt you. As adults we can choose a different, better way.

Note: In order to protect the privacy of clients, family members, friends, and others, I have changed the names and specific circumstances of all the individuals mentioned throughout this book.

1 THE TIES THAT BIND

After two stressful and often unhappy years of marriage, Mike and Jennifer were ready to file for divorce. However, before they rushed off to lawyers, a friend of the couple's convinced them to try counseling and referred them to me. I saw this couple many years ago, when I was fairly new to family therapy, but even so, I had already seen many couples whose problems initially appeared far more serious than Mike and Jennifer's. I anticipated a reasonably simple resolution to their difficulties. How wrong I was.

Mike and Jennifer were extremely angry and hostile to each other, virtually unable to agree on anything. It would be months before we could consider solutions to their problems. So what went wrong so early in their relationship?

I Didn't Expect to Marry Your Mother!

When we met for our first appointment, Mike took the lead in telling their sad story. He loved Jennifer deeply, he said, and had hoped to spend the rest of his life happily married to her. But, and this was a very big but, he never expected to spend the rest of his life with his mother-in-law, Ethyl.

When he was truthful with himself and with Jennifer, he admitted that he couldn't stand his mother-in-law, had never liked her, not from the first moment he had met her. On a verbal roll now, he described her as exceptionally loud, extremely bossy, overly critical, and interfering, to boot.

Meanwhile, as she listened to Mike go on and on, Jennifer burst into tears. When she could gather herself together to speak, she agreed that her mother could be unpleasant. But, "She's my *mother* and I *love* her. If I ask her not to come over to our house, she'll be *hurt*."

At this point I asked Jennifer how often her mother visited their home. "Well," she said, "almost every day." Mike shot me an "I-rest-my-case" look.

Over the next weeks and months, the full story emerged. It seemed that Jennifer had been close to her mother all her life. She thought of her as a friend, and they did just about everything together, from cooking gourmet meals to shopping for clothes. She depended on her mother's advice, and she admitted, a bit sheepishly, that she wouldn't even buy a sweater without her mother's approval of the color and style.

What about women friends? Did Jennifer have a circle of women to confide in or to go out with from time to time? Unlike most women, Jennifer had a limited number of friends with whom she talked about personal things. Her mother had always played that role in her life, and she didn't feel the need to seek other significant relationships.

Once Jennifer met Mike, she spent private time with him, of course, but she continued to see her mother whenever she could. This went on even after the wedding, which was a situation Mike hadn't bargained for. In actuality, Jennifer didn't care much for her in-laws, and she could understand why Mike didn't like Ethyl, who, she admitted, could be difficult. But she hadn't taken Mike's serious dislike of her mother to heart. In fact, she and Mike had shared a few laughs over typical—and popular—mother-in-law jokes.

But neither was now laughing when they sat in my office, angry and hostile. Mike and Jennifer had hard work ahead of them, work that probably should have been done long before they took their trip to the altar.

The Way It Should Be

Two people meet, they fall in love, and one day they decide to spend the rest of their lives together. Ideally, our two partners are mature, capable of forming a close and committed bond. The couple live a comfortable distance from their parents and have had independent lives for a few years, whether away at college or while starting careers. As they look forward to their marriage, they anticipate a good relationship with both families, although they know it will be more distant. This particular couple understand that their primary commitment is to each other and to the children they may have in the future.

While the change may be subtle, they realize that their loyalties will shift. Neither will automatically drop everything just because a parent calls or requests something. Nor will they spend *all* their time with their siblings. While they will develop independent interests and they may include their parents and siblings in certain activities, they know the family ties will change. They have spent considerable time discussing their feelings about their families.

When the first holidays come around, this couple already know how they intend to handle conflicting demands on their time. They have agreed to compromise, and they stick to their agreements; if the in-law families are angry, then so be it. They do their best to smooth over hurt feelings, and when they can't, they turn to each other and talk the situation through. Sometimes, they must agree to disagree, but being two mature individuals, committed to each other, they can cope with some dissension.

Sometimes one or both of the people in our ideal couple lives at home with parents before marrying, and so looks forward to the privacy they will have in a home of their own. Some young people may even anticipate that escaping from domineering or interfering parents is a benefit of marriage. They may expect to have loving, close relationships with parents and siblings, but they will turn to each other for most of the emotional support they need.

What does this new relationship, the creation of a new family, look like from the parents-in-law point of view? Some in-laws may breathe a sigh of relief when a child marries. They look forward to living more carefree lives, with fewer bills, fewer worries. They may even get a good laugh at the old joke, "Life begins when the dog dies and the kids leave home." When they see their children—and grandchildren—they're pleased, but they don't count on continuing the same relationship they had in the past. They have some lingering doubts about their child's choice of a spouse, but oh well, the kids have to make their own choices and mistakes, if a mistake is what the marriage turns out to be.

The above scenario is probably an ideal for most of us. This is the way family relationships should flow when all goes well. However, for Jennifer and Mike, and millions of other people, the reality falls far short of this idealized version of family ties.

The Way It Often Is

Marriage is viewed as a normal part of the life cycle—children grow up, leave home, marry, produce children, and so forth. Sometimes they marry and move far away, and many couples don't have children, by choice or by circumstance.

In any case, a new family is created, a unit that operates autonomously. But in our culture we have a common saying: "You not only marry your mate; you marry the whole family, too." And while we like to think that both the young married couple and their respective families are mature, rational people, often this is not the case. Our family of origin influences and shapes our expectations and attitudes more than most of us ever imagine. When a young couple (or even an older couple, perhaps marrying for the second time) do not anticipate problems and agree on solutions before the touchy situations arise, trouble just naturally occurs. Far too often, everyone involved takes a "head in the sand" approach and hopes that all this bickering will just go away.

I can look to my own life experience for examples of the way parent and in-law relationships affect the marriage bond. In fact, extended family problems took quite a toll on my own marriage before we resolved them—which didn't happen overnight. My own situation, combined with the work I've done with my clients, led me to further examine the life cycle of the in-law relationship. After all, in many, if not most, situations, this relationship starts even before the engagement is announced. And then comes the stress of planning a wedding, followed by the inevitable adjustments all concerned must make in the first few years of a new marriage.

Working with couples increased my awareness of how common in-law problems are in typical marriages. Add to that the influences, both positive and negative, that we all bring from our own nuclear families into our marriages, and we have set the stage for conflict. The intense feelings surrounding family issues often result in major confrontations, deep wounds, and extreme unhappiness for individuals, couples, and extended families.

Not all parents are happy to see a child leave home, even when they are fond of the person their child is marrying. Some parents don't want to let go of the ties that bind them to their children. Rather than looking ahead to years of freedom and perhaps the joy of grandchildren, these parents dislike their empty nest.

Similarly, not all grown children want to loosen the ties that bind them to their parents and siblings, nor are they eager to add in-law family members to their circle of affection. The biggest problems occur when the couple hasn't talked about these issues and, therefore, reacts to conflict as if it came from nowhere—out of the blue. Yet, in every case I have seen (including my own), the warning signs, the red flags, were there all along, usually waving wildly in the breeze, begging for attention.

Picture this: Natalie was the bride. She chose as one of her bridesmaids a sister-in-law she didn't speak to. But Natalie's fiancé had insisted that his sister, Betts, be "a member of the wedding." So Natalie and Betts went down the same aisle on the wedding day and then spent the whole evening at this long-anticipated and supposedly joyous event without speaking so much as one word to each other. Guests, most of whom were unaware of the situation, wondered why so many angry looks passed between the two young women all night long.

Or consider Myra, who cut out the pictures of her mother-in-law in her wedding album, ruining the expensive and lovely remembrance of her special day. Myra disliked her mother-in-law, Edna, so intensely that she would not allow her to set foot in her house under any circumstances. She drew her blinds and never answered the door if she thought the dreaded Edna was on the way. Just imagine how this hostility affected Myra's relationship with her husband. Is she naive enough to believe that this destructive situation with her mother-in-law doesn't have the potential to destroy her marriage? Unfortunately, many people are just this naive.

B UT **naïveté shows up in many ways.** One woman—an attractive, professional in her fifties—sat in my office wringing her hands as she said, "I just can't understand how my son can be so completely involved with this woman [his wife], especially when you think of all the years of devoted attention I've given him. He doesn't stop at my house to see me after work anymore—he used to come almost every day. Doesn't she know he has an obligation to his mother—doesn't she know I was there first?"

Fortunately for her daughter-in-law, this woman's son understood that when he married, the tie to his mother had to loosen significantly. It was the only healthy way for him to establish a new family. As is typical in these situations, this woman blames her son's wife, failing to place responsibility on him or to look at herself. In line with the archetype of "daughter-in-law," Mom thought the young woman was a mini-witch who seduced her son away from her. Few people want to admit that they have those feelings, but I see them every day. Countless people fail to untie the bindings that hold them to their families of origin and to their children.

Learning to Untie the Knots

In the natural order of things, the ties to one's original family are usually bound tightly. It must be so. These tight bindings allow a baby to grow into an independent child, one who eventually leaves home and assumes adult responsibilities. When the ties are too loose or broken too early, insecurity and other personality difficulties are often the sad result.

Most people, however, don't give much thought to how these ties with their family of origin will change as they move toward adulthood. While the engagement period logically could be the appropriate time to consider these inevitable changes, often a kind of glow exists around the couple. In these happy, positive days, many people are reluctant to consider future problems. We might say that some people go through a period during which they are viewing their future through "rose-colored glasses."

Other people, however, feel threatened and jealous during this busy time and could greatly benefit from heartfelt talks to sort out the budding problems—before the wedding. They could avoid future ugliness in the marriage and in the extended family if they faced the problems before they escalate.

If you are looking forward to getting married, I urge you to discuss the expectations about future relationships with the in-law family right now. Don't wait just because things seem so good at this point. Conversely, don't *hope* that current tensions will iron themselves out later. From what I've seen, that won't happen. You might find yourself sitting in a therapist's office, like Mike and Jennifer, wondering where and why it all went wrong.

If even a hint of trouble lurks between you and your in-law-family-to-be and you and your future spouse are having difficulty talking about it, much less working through your attitudes and expectations, then I believe pre-marital counseling is in order. Head off those problems now. The information presented in this book tells you what can happen when you ignore family problems. Preventing a problem is far easier than facing the work involved in searching for a solution years later, when the damage is done.

Tangled Expectations

When she met her future in-laws for the first time, Karen thought they were open and friendly. What a relief that was. Karen hadn't seen her own parents in several years; their negativity and narrow-mindedness had driven her crazy, and she walked away from them rather than continuing to try to resolve the problems.

Karen was looking forward to being part of a family that was harmonious, and she was pleased that her future in-laws appeared to welcome her happily into the family. No one was more surprised than Karen when she ended up in a therapist's office six months after the wedding. These once warm, welcoming people were now nosy and interfering. She complained to her new husband, Larry, about them almost every day, and within weeks of the wedding, she was behaving coldly toward them.

Larry reacted to his wife's nasty comments by jumping to his parents' defense. He was becoming increasingly angry with Karen, whom he now accused of being jealous of his good family relationships. And so the battle raged, getting hotter by the day. By the time they came to counseling, they were a bewildered and sad pair.

Both spouses had much to learn about their feelings and reactions to their problems, and the insight they needed had to come from examining the memories and experiences they brought from their families of origin. Neither fully understood that we all bring with us to our marriage strong emotional attachments—or even the lack of them—from our birth families. We do not recreate ourselves when we get married. Rather, we're blending two people's disparate experiences, traditions, customs, belief systems, and psychological baggage. And we expect it all to go smoothly? Rarely is this so.

As this couple worked on their issues, I heard Larry describe his need to be involved with his family because he felt so close to them. Until he married, at age thirty-six, he had lived happily at home. His mother had cooked all his meals, washed his clothes, and taken care of all his other physical comforts. He had talked with his parents about personal and professional issues and relied on their advice and support.

Well-meaning relatives and friends had warned Larry about this unhealthy dependency and advised him to learn to take care of himself and do things on his own. Larry didn't heed this advice because he couldn't accept that he was spoiled and not a fully grown adult. His parents liked their arrangement, so why shouldn't he?

Karen's story was much different. She had been on her own since age eighteen, having left her indifferent and obviously dysfunctional home environment. She and her parents had disagreed so often about so much that she couldn't wait to get away. In time, Karen would admit that she was jealous of Larry's relationship with his parents. In addition, she admitted that she was afraid that her husband was basically a "mamma's boy" and would never be able to completely commit to her. After all, she thought, if he was so attached to them, how could he become deeply attached to her? Karen's family had obvious problems that she freely admitted. Larry, on the other hand, wouldn't admit that his relationship with his parents was also dysfunctional in some ways.

This couple was fortunate in that they truly loved each other and wanted to understand what had gone wrong. They deeply wanted to fix their relationship and restore a happy bond between them. If they hadn't shown that commitment, the marriage would have continued its downhill slide. Karen would have ended up believing that no one could be trusted to really love her, and Larry would have returned to the familiar emotional climate of his parents' home.

Karen and Larry are a good example of the way we all bring "baggage" to our relationships. Part of the baggage—a large part—includes ideas and expectations of marriage and family life. These experiences include the mental and emotional ways families function. Families give us our first education about values, morals, and expectations about relationships. Later on, we are exposed to other influences, from media to clergy to friends. Nowadays, we have "authorities" and "experts," those people who for one reason or another lay claim to special knowledge about various psychological issues. By the time we reach late adolescence and early adulthood, we have many ideas solidly—some might say rigidly—formed.

Since no one ever marries his or her clone, we all bring a different set of life and marriage values into a new relationship. We see how these attitudes and expectations affect relationships with new friends, business associates, and even neighbors. It shouldn't come as a big surprise that these same issues are brought into our marriages and may even be a source of conflict. Yet, because we don't prepare for the difficulties (foolishly believing that love conquers all), we are often surprised when they arise.

Larry and Karen were able to resolve their problems through understanding and compromise. When Karen expressed her envy of a close family tie, her concern about Larry's ability to form a close tie with her made more sense to her husband. Larry felt less threatened when he realized that Karen didn't expect him to turn his back on his family, but rather, she just wanted some compromise. She wanted him to turn to her as a confidant, something he was willing to do, and she wished that he would set the boundaries with his family on his own. The last thing she wanted was to look like the villain (the little witch who stole a son) to his family. Larry was willing to do this if Karen would make an effort to enjoy the more limited time they spent with his parents. Karen agreed to try to build a few bridges with her own family, realizing that unresolved issues would continue to affect her—and now her marriage as well.

The ending for this couple has been a happy one. But feelings were hurt all around in Larry's family. His sister feels betrayed, and his mother feels abandoned. "Our Larry doesn't come around much—he seems to prefer *her*." But Larry and Karen have made big strides toward true maturity.

Adding Changing Roles and Diversity to the Mix

Karen and Larry were the same race, they practiced the same religion, they had grown up in similar economic circumstances, they were educated about equally, and both had been reared in the early years by stay-at-home mothers. Experts might say they were sociologically well matched. Yet look at the problems they brought to their relationship. Just imagine the potential problems when a marriage *doesn't* follow such neat patterns. Our society is a rich cultural stew, and no one knows what will happen next! Let's look at some small—and big—examples of the kind of challenges we currently face as society and the family structure change.

What? Me—Wash Dishes?

Rachel was tired from working all day and making a trip to the daycare center to pick up two-year-old Kimmy. Rob usually came home just about the time she was cooking dinner. He played with the baby for a little while and then turned on the news. Within minutes he was asleep, at which point Rachel usually let him rest while she gave Kimmy her dinner, bathed her, read her a bedtime story, and settled her into bed. Then Rachel returned to the kitchen, put dinner on the table, woke Rob up, and told him dinner was ready.

Rachel couldn't help but comment on her fatigue—she hadn't had a minute of rest all day. Sometimes Rob feigned interest, but more often, he didn't appear to care. One night he was in a bad mood, but Rachel was so tired she didn't notice. When she got up from the table, she said, "Thank goodness it's your night to do the dishes—I'm exhausted."

Rob exploded. "I'm not doing the lousy dishes—I'm tired of being a housewife around here. My father never washed the dishes, and my mother stayed home and raised the kids like you're supposed to do. By the time you pay for daycare, there isn't even enough money left to make working worthwhile anyway. Just quit the damned job and stay home and do what God intended a woman to do!"

The first time Rob launched into this diatribe, Rachel was stunned. But by this point, she was no longer even surprised at his outbursts. Now the argument, which had started shortly after the baby was born, was typical. Several times they had tried to talk it out, but the bottom line was the same. Rob strongly believed a woman's place was in the home and, therefore, Rachel's job was to take care of him and their children. (He used God to shore up his position.) Dishwashing was by definition Rachel's job.

Rachel had had a different role model. Her mother had raised three children while holding a responsible job that gave her great personal satisfaction. Rachel and her two brothers admired their mother and their father as well. He had been an active parent and had done a fair share of the work around their childhood home. Rachel believed she could have a good marriage, do a good job raising children, and have a successful career. She just wanted Rob to be a full partner. Was that too much to ask?

Rob and Rachel are bumping up against the relatively new problem of defining roles. Career women are not a new reality, and many such women have been fortunate enough to have husbands who understood equality and carried a share of the family's practical workload. Other women have had to work harder to juggle their various hats because they had little support from husbands or other family members. Sometimes people harken back to the fifties and wish for June and Ward Cleaver to return. If the family portrayed on 1950s television ever was a reality for most people, which is doubtful, it certainly is not going to resume in our era.

IN my practice I've seen the ways in which the role changes have affected family life and how conflicting expectations spill over into in-law relationships. In some cases, in-law families are living the changes brought us by the women's movement and shifting economic conditions. I've heard mothers-in-law complain that their son's wife is lazy because she wants to stay home with the new baby. I've heard others describe their daughter-in-law as selfish because she wants to go back to work rather than stay home where she belongs. Not surprisingly, Rob's mother took this position, cheered on by his father.

You might be astonished to learn that Rob and Rachel had never discussed this issue before they were married.

Rachel's life had been greatly influenced by the women's movement. Both her mother and her father were active in the early years of the struggle for women's equality. Rachel's great-grandmother had been a proud and feisty suffragist. To say that Rachel didn't understand Rob's attitudes is an understatement.

When I worked with this couple, Rob expressed deep shame that, by his family's standards, he didn't "wear the pants," and because he finally admitted to shame, rather than just anger, Rachel tried to listen to him. Before this she had dismissed his feelings as the ravings of a selfish chauvinist. (Many women would—Rachel is not alone.) In order for their marriage to move forward, both were going to need to listen to each other and attempt to understand where their two different sets of attitudes came from. They still have a very long way to go. Down deep, each has an entirely different vision of family life. They may or may not be able to work it out, but they now know that they should have talked about these issues before the wedding.

What Is a Family Anyway?

Fraught with deep religious and political divisions, the definition of family remains an open issue. The so-called two-parent-based family isn't necessarily the norm today—at least in many people's eyes. Marianne, a divorced mother with children living with her is a family; the father, Hal, considers himself and his children a family too, even though they can't spend time together every day or even every week. Jody and Bill each have a child, and all four live together in a step-family, or as it is commonly called today, a blended family. They believe they're a family, but they admit the in-law situation can get fairly complicated. The biological grandparents sometimes interact with step-grandparents, which can be tricky, especially at family gatherings.

Also consider Brenda and Libby, plus their two children. They have a loving lesbian relationship, and they believe they constitute a family. Ron and Jeffrey are a family, too, even though the law will not allow them to marry. They have parents who function much like the in-laws heterosexual couples have. One set approves of their relationship, while the other set struggles to come to terms with it. In addition, their siblings are all over the map about this gay union.

Mary is a single mother who decided to have a child without having the baby's biological father involved. She believes that she and her daughter are a family. In her case, she has a sister-in-law, her brother's wife, who neither likes her nor approves of her single-mom-never-married status. My friend Hillary has never married, but she has a favorite nephew who lives nearby with his new wife. She thinks she is part of her nephew's new family. The unresolved question is how close the couple care to be to this "aunt-in-law." So far, the expectations of the aunt appear to be quite different from those of the new couple.

Add to these nontraditional arrangements Rose and Paul, a couple in their eighties who live together and have no intention of marrying, much to their children's dismay. We even see groups of people, single mothers and their children, for example, who say they are a family, while their parents may prefer to think of them as a big group of friends.

No simple, or single, definition of "family" exists today, no matter how disapproving others are of the variety of arrangements and commitments spread widely across our country of 260 million people. If we hope that clashes among family members will go away by withholding recognition of this array of different arrangements, then we waste our time.

Most families will find peace only if they dig in and work on the issues that divide them.

Gay Is Okay—But Must You Talk About It?

At age twenty-nine, Joyce mustered up the courage to tell her parents that she is a lesbian. The decision to reveal the truth about this one part of her life came after considerable anguish and heartache. She knew her family would be unhappy, possibly even outraged and rejecting, when they learned about her sexual orientation. Her fears were justified because at first they were distant and very cold, skirting the border of out-and-out rejection.

It took several years before it appeared that Joyce's family was willing to reconcile and truly accept Joyce's choices. Eventually, they seemed to become accustomed to their daughter and her partner, and no one even mentioned it anymore. All this goodwill changed when Joyce and her partner decided to have a marriage ceremony, even though it would be a ritual without legal sanction. The two women planned to send invitations to both extended families.

This proved too much for Joyce's family, who it turned out had never really accepted her relationship with her partner and had been repressing a great deal of animosity for years. They explained that they expected Joyce to keep her lifestyle a secret—in other words, her sexual orientation was okay as long as no one knew about it outside the small nuclear family. And a wedding? Don't be ridiculous. Inviting relatives was out of the question.

The arguments escalated, and one night Joyce felt compelled to walk away from her family after her parents and siblings expressed their real feelings. At the present time, Joyce hasn't spoken with any relative for several months. It is likely that this family tie will remain broken for the foreseeable future. Because Joyce is upset, her partner is too. This may be an unusual parent and in-law problem, but think about all the men and women who are estranged from their families. Gay couples may not have such different problems after all.

Living in "Sin"

Amy and David are having difficulty with their families and this couple isn't even married. Amy's parents are very displeased that she is living with David and believe she is foolish to make it easy for David to "reap the benefits of marriage" without a permanent commitment (however "permanent" is defined these days). David's parents have a different take on this; they think Amy is a tramp, reflective of their adherence to the old-time double standard for men and women.

At first David and Amy just laughed off all this disapproval and enjoyed themselves. They had other friends who lived together, and those young people didn't feel guilty, so why should they? This sounds simple, but it isn't. They find themselves in frequent arguments about their families, and Amy is having trouble being with her parents because she feels criticized and diminished in their presence. Meanwhile, she is furious with David's parents, who avoid her company; they treat her as if she has a communicable disease.

As time goes on, the bloom on the rose is beginning to fade for Amy. What if her family is right? She was raised in a religion that doesn't approve of sex before marriage, and her parents won't budge on those values. David's parents, she sometimes thinks, just might be right. She wonders if David might have absorbed his parents' values, too. One day, will he consider her a tramp? This couple are now in deep trouble. Family-of-origin influence can't be overstated.

He Practices What? Or, She Calls God Who?

When I was growing up, marrying outside my religion was unthinkable. No one even discussed such a possibility. Most of my friends were raised the same way. But the world changes, and now Robert and Betty, a Catholic and a Muslim, are unable to communicate with either set of parents. Fortunately, they have open-minded siblings, or this couple would have completely broken previous family ties. The parents of two preschool children, Robert and Betty long for their parents to see their beautiful family. Their respective brothers and sisters have tried to reason with the parents. They enthusiastically tell stories about how well the marriage is going and how nicely they've blended their religious traditions. But it's all to no avail. One of their friends recently quipped, "Well, at least you don't have interfering in-laws the way I do." Everyone laughed, but as a long-term advantage, it leaves much to be desired.

Mamma, Meet My Girl

David called his mom, Rebecca, and said, "I'm bringing home my fiancée. She's beautiful and wonderful, but don't be shocked—she's an Indian." Rebecca *was* shocked but thought she had to make the best of it and at least meet this mystery woman.

David brought the girl home and introduced her. She was indeed a Native American, complete with native garb and a long thick braid down her back. She held out her hand to Rebecca and said, "Hi. I'm Running Water." Without skipping a beat, Rebecca replied, "Hi. I'm Sitting Shiva."

As far as I know, this is not a true story; it's actually a joke I heard a few years ago. Sitting shiva is a Jewish custom, part of the mourning ritual for the dead. It's significant because many a Jewish parent has been known to say that he or she would feel as if the child had died if a son or daughter dared to marry outside the faith. As awful as it sounds, some Orthodox Jews really do demand that this ritual be carried out when a child marries a non-Jewish person. Thankfully, not too many people go to this extreme about intermarriage, whether the issue is religion or race or ethnicity.

Petty, Petty, Petty

Our society may be increasingly tolerant about many of the larger social issues, but the talk shows are still filled with programs about the various reasons parents disapprove of a child's choice of a partner. Some reasons are excuses; these parents wouldn't approve of anyone. Imagine rejecting a future daughter-in-law because she isn't pretty enough or because her parents aren't well-educated, which is translated into the tactless term, "stupid." One woman didn't like her future son-in-law because he dressed too casually; another thought the music her daughter's boyfriend played as a hobby was "tacky." One woman made fun of her future sister-in-law because she was "too fat." You get the idea.

When all kinds of bogus reasons are given to reject a child's or sibling's choice, the ties that bind can become fragile indeed. Sometimes a person will attempt to walk the middle road and support both a future partner and the family. But sometimes, the families remain enemies forever, and I've seen heartbreaking divorces result. Most of the time the critical family, which contributed to the problems in the first place, will smugly say, "I knew *she* wasn't right for him" or "What did I tell you? I knew she'd come to her senses and get rid of that bum." It takes very special people to withstand the kind of stress that truly rejecting families heap on a couple.

I Thought She Was Perfect But Now, I'm Not So Sure . . .

There's an old story about a man who brings his bride-to-be home to meet his family. He's so proud of his beautiful girl—she's tall, voluptuous, and oh, so smart. His family is polite to her but when she leaves, one sister says, "She has such crooked teeth," and another adds, "She looks like she'll be really fat one day—just wait 'til she has kids." The mother nods her head and says, "Such a tall girl—she shouldn't wear those high heels." The father is compelled to add his two cents and comments, "And her grammar—she must have common parents."

The next time our young man sees his girlfriend, he notices that her bottom teeth are a bit crooked, and ouch, she used the wrong word in a sentence. Boy, she sure ate a big dinner, plus dessert, and he never realized that she is almost as tall as he is. By the end of the evening, his girl isn't quite as beautiful or smart as he had once believed. And, heaven forbid, all those voluptuous curves might just turn to fat one day. Too bad, she just isn't right for him anymore. Thank goodness he found out in time.

Ken thought he was in love with Chrissy, and he adored her two children. At thirty-seven, he was ready for marriage, and he even liked the idea of a ready-made family. He couldn't have been more delighted with the way his life was going. Ken eagerly arranged for his family to meet the three new loves of his life. Poor guy. He was taken aback at how cool his parents and two sisters were toward Chrissy. He had thought they would love her immediately, just the way he had.

Chrissy went off to use the bathroom, and the comments started. She certainly wasn't good enough for him, and why was she divorced? Was she a bad wife? Why on earth would

Ken want a woman who was a failure? Her first marriage had failed, hadn't it? And marriage is so difficult—two kids that aren't even his will make it that much harder, and didn't he realize how much kids cost? Why should their darling son and brother be stuck supporting two strangers? As handsome and successful as he was, he could do much better. He could have any woman he wanted. (The family failed to acknowledge that Ken seemed to have difficulty making a lasting connection with any woman.) Since they couldn't find any way to like her, it was going to be rough going, these "loving" relatives claimed. This Chrissy woman just wasn't their type and certainly wouldn't fit in. Impossible.

Like most people, Ken reacted defensively. He loved Chrissy. She was a wonderful mother, and her first husband had cheated on her and run off with his secretary. She hadn't failed. That night, he left with Chrissy, determined not to let their irrational prejudices ruin his happiness: great resolve, but alas, no follow-through. Gradually, his family wore him down, and he broke his engagement. His family, he thought, must know best, which was the only comfort he had as he walked away from Chrissy and her children. Now, years later, he's still not married, and he thinks about what a fool he was to let Chrissy go. She's found someone else, so it's too late. He really lost her.

Ken sounds like a bit of a dope, but let's not be too harsh. Are you certain you would have bucked your family? After all, they had statistics on their side. Blended families do have a hard time, and being a step-father isn't easy. Besides, second marriages don't have a greater chance for success than first marriages. I worked with Ken for over a year, and it took him many sessions before he understood that his biggest problem was an inability to follow his heart.

When he went back to the point of his decision, he realized that he'd let the pressure of others guide his decisions, even when his heart had said that Chrissy was right for him. In my first book, *When the Wrong Thing Is Right,* I discuss the importance of learning to follow one's intuition —one's heart—when making important life choices. We'll never know, but Ken might have found happiness with Chrissy and her children. He did the so-called right thing by taking his parents' advice when they said the marriage would start out with built-in problems. But letting Chrissy go was wrong for him—his heart never let him forget it. Even if the marriage had failed for some reason, it would have been his own mistake, and he would have taken responsibility for it.

Following Your Heart as You Get Untied

The loyalties we have to our family of origin are often very strong, and as we've seen, sometimes too powerful. In order to make our own choices and develop the relationships we want in our new families, we must accommodate new stages in family life. If we're parents-in-law, we must adjust to our children's choice of a mate and accept that our dear darlings, those kids we invested so much in, are forming their own families now, and we may be very surprised at the composition of this new unit. Maybe we approve of some things our children do and disapprove of others, but for the most part, we no longer have a voice in our grown children's lives.

If we're the people moving away from the close family ties, we may have to accept that breaking the bonds may not always be easy. Perhaps our future spouse makes a negative comment about our brother or sister. She or he may not like one or both of our parents and absolutely loathes our step-father. Oh dear. We better talk about this and get it all out in the open, because it isn't going to get better by itself.

Some of these struggles are a natural part of getting untied from the bonds of the family of origin. Are the struggles worth it? For the most part, it serves us well to try to work things out. In-law relationships can be healthy and add a new dimension to our lives. We can achieve great personal growth when we work toward understanding and harmony. While I realize that sometimes a situation can be so hopeless that permanent estrangement from family members is the only way to keep the marriage harmonious, this is an extreme situation, not to mention unacceptable for most couples and their families.

The most important advice I can offer is this: Understand that the in-law relationship is fluid, not static. The situation you're dealing with today may change tomorrow. You'll have one kind of relationship with in-laws or in-law children in one decade and an entirely different kind ten years later. In addition, the quality of this relationship depends largely on your understanding of the expectations you carry with you from your family of origin. Once you achieve some insight, you may find the accommodations and adjustments you need to make far easier.

In the next chapter, we'll take a look at issues that are present before the wedding plans even begin. Unfortunately, we often don't see in-law problems during the courtship as true problems, so we spend too little time trying to solve them. But the life cycle of the in-law relationship starts before the wedding and often offers a snapshot view of what is ahead. One doesn't need a crystal ball to see the future—eyes and ears will suffice in this fortune-telling exercise.

2 IS THIS HOW IT'S GOING TO BE?

Some years ago I witnessed an unforgettable scene on one of the popular daytime talk shows. The theme for the day was "mothers who dislike their son's fiancées." One engaged couple, together with the young man's mother, were in deep trouble—and the wedding was still months off. Lest you think this was a dispute over the bride being of a different religion or race, or a belief that the couple was too young to marry, or some such issue, let me explain clearly that nothing of the slightest importance was involved. The couple practiced the same religion, came from the same ethnic background, and both were college graduates.

I don't remember their names, but let's call this trio Sue, Sam, and Cheryl. In the twenty minutes or so that the couple was featured, Sue and Cheryl argued over such earth-shaking issues as the quality of Sue's spaghetti sauce and who did a better job of ironing Sam's shirts. The young couple had gone to grammar school together, and Sam's mother, Cheryl, had known Sue all her life. It wasn't that she disliked Sue; well, not exactly. It was just that she was convinced her son could find a "better" woman—whatever that means. Sue's family wasn't quite as well educated as Cheryl and her husband, and the mother-in-law-to-be criticized the career path Sue had chosen. (Cheryl was a stay-at-home mom, but somehow Sue wasn't climbing the corporate ladder fast enough for her mother-in-law-to-be. Go figure.)

With Sam sitting in the middle, Cheryl ranted on about Sue's cooking (not as good as hers), Sue's hairstyle (not classy enough), her inability to iron Sam's shirts correctly (a fact Sue tearfully argued—this was the ultimate humiliation), and on and on. Sam never said a word. Finally, the host commented that the young man seemed to enjoy having two women fight over who could take better care of him. Sam grinned, with only a touch of sheepishness on his face. Soon, other people in the audience began challenging Sam to stand up for his bride-to-be, to tell his mother to stop criticizing and leave them alone. One person remarked that this duel over whose spaghetti sauce was better was truly infantile, but Sam commented only that his mother's sauce was a tad better. The audience groaned. Sam was hopeless. Here were two grown women competing over the privilege of catering to him, and he sat back and enjoyed the ride.

Was this a couple headed for trouble? I'll say they were. They were in trouble for many reasons, but the biggest problem was sitting in the middle basking in the attention. Sam thought he was Prince Sam, whose every wish should be granted. Cheryl treated her husband like a king and her son like a prince. In her household, the daughters served the men. Needless to say, Sam's sisters left home early, but Sam had no need to move away. He didn't even see that this rivalry over taking care of him was problematic.

For her part, Sue was not challenging the premise that Sam should be pampered. She just wanted the privilege of doing it herself, without interference from her mother-in-law-to-be. And Cheryl was determined not to let go. No woman would ever be good enough for her son. As if this weren't bad enough, she had raised Sam with a sense of entitlement. He expected women to anticipate his needs, and as a result, he had stayed a selfish little boy.

Will the Prince Ever Grow Up?

As much as things have changed in our culture, some things stay the same. In most families, the women are responsible for maintaining family relationships. Who in your family remembers all the birthdays and anniversaries? Who keeps track of the holiday plans, what each family should bring, and who should be invited? A woman is often expected to pay attention to her husband's parents, but a man is not necessarily expected to put the same kind of emotional energy into establishing a relationship with his in-laws. This happens because women are still expected to take care of relationships, even when this arrangement has never been defined in words. But it is an assumption that many young —and not so young—people carry into their marriages. Often these expectations are part of the baggage we bring to relationships.

In many families, the boys still are treated differently from the girls. Most situations are not as extreme as in Cheryl's household, but the seeds of future problems are sown when the boys in the family aren't raised to be full-grown men, able to take care of themselves and be true partners in a marriage. Sue believes that if she is going to make Sam happy, she has to compete with Cheryl; she must outdo her mother-in-law at her own caregiving game. Like many women, Sue is preparing to carry more of the load of the marriage, on both practical and emotional levels.

In the glow of young love, this can all be wrapped in a

cloak of romance, resulting in the attitude that "I'll do any-thing for the one I love." As the months and years pass, however, few women are able to tolerate critical in-laws and a husband who won't bond so completely with her that he is able to loosen the strong ties he has with his parents. Yet his marriage may depend on doing just that. Rather than the prince turning into a king he needs to turn into a grown-up man. I wish this were as easy as it sounds.

The Princess in the Tower

Sometimes women are raised to be taken care of, perhaps in ways different from men, but that are just as real. In this situation, it is the young women who have a difficult time growing up and separating from their parents. Often, a dot-ing father is at the heart of the problem.

Research in the last couple of decades has confirmed that successful women often have fathers who appreciate and affirm their daughters' intelligence and capabilities. These fathers are proud of their daughters' good grades, assertive-ness, and accomplishments. In other words, the daughters of affirming fathers believe that being independent thinkers capable of making their way in the world is compatible with femininity.

Sometimes, however, the messages can become confused, and rather than becoming independent, the daughter ends up a princess. In these cases, fatherly protectiveness is dis-torted and becomes unhealthy indulgence. Sometimes these young women don't grow up and break the ties with dot-ing Daddy, and their husbands are expected to carry on the indulgence. This can have tragic results because the woman hasn't grown up and loosened her ties to a father who believes in his heart that nothing is too good for his little girl.

Nat is a wealthy lawyer who takes great pleasure in

giving his family the very best he can afford. His wife and children have lived in the lap of luxury, wanting for nothing. From clothes to cars to jewelry, they've had everything money can buy. Nat loves his two sons, but he is wild about his only daughter, Betsy. He admits that he has pampered and spoiled his "little princess." He was thrilled when she decided to become a lawyer, too. Of course, she needed a new sports car, and student housing wasn't good enough for Betsy, so he signed a lease for a spacious condo near the law school and hired a decorator to furnish it.

Shortly after she passed the bar exam, Betsy married Jon, whom she'd known from her high school days. Nat tried to discourage the marriage because he thought there had to be "better catches out there." Betsy didn't listen to her father; she was used to getting what she wanted, and she wanted Jon.

Jon was an intelligent young man, and he sensed that Nat didn't think he was good enough for Betsy. The messages were clear enough. Polite and cordial on the surface, the relationship was slowly poisoned by the constant undercurrents of hostility and disapproval.

Betsy had two babies right away, and she and Jon agreed that she should stay home with them and delay starting her law career. Jon was still struggling with his career, and with Betsy not working, they could afford only a weekly cleaning person. But Daddy couldn't have that. Like many mothers, Betsy was tired from taking care of two babies, and Daddy thought she needed more help. So, he hired a full-time nanny and a maid that came in every other day. Jon was uncomfortable with this financial dependency, but he wanted Betsy to be happy, so he kept his feelings to himself.

The years passed, and Nat continued his generosity to his daughter and the grandchildren. Betsy said that the house was getting small, so he made a large down payment on a bigger house. Jon tried to say no, but he gave in because his wife wanted it so badly. Increasingly, he felt like an outsider rather than a true partner. Jon wanted a new house too, but he wanted to work with Betsy on a plan to buy it in two years. He would have liked to take vacations with Betsy and the children, but he was working hard to get ahead in his career and couldn't take much time off. Nat insisted that Betsy and the children take vacations without Jon, and Betsy sided with her father. How could Jon be selfish and deny her a good time?

So were the princess and her two men headed for trouble? You bet. In truth, they were in trouble before the ink on the marriage certificate was dry. Jon spent more and more time quietly seething. Resentful and angry, he tried to talk to Betsy about how he felt, but she just didn't understand. Why should she be denied just because he didn't make enough money to satisfy her desires? Daddy loved indulging her—why should she deprive him of that pleasure?

This couple came to me for counseling because Jon had become involved with another woman. At one time, he said, this would have been unthinkable, because he and Betsy were devoted to each other. But the more he felt pushed away and sensed he was not important to her, the more tempting turning to another woman for comfort and affirmation became.

Initially, Jon did most of the talking while Betsy tried, for the first time, to listen carefully. Her husband felt unworthy and inferior, and the frustration had been building for years. He loved her, but it seemed that she would only truly love him if he could give her every material advantage and luxury she was used to. So the "other woman" was not important in the long run, but she had helped him feel good about himself, and she genuinely cared about his feelings. Jon wanted his marriage to work and promised that his lapse in judgment would never happen again.

Betsy was willing to forgive Jon, and she even admitted that she'd probably undermined her husband's self-confidence and hadn't formed an independent family unit with him. She agreed that she'd taken too many gifts from her father. Nat, who had jumped in at this sign of trouble and agreed to pay for a divorce, realized that his daughter wanted her marriage to work and said he'd stop being part of the problem. He said that he loved his daughter enough to stop giving her so much! Progress at last.

Unfortunately, saying and doing are two different things. Betsy had a difficult time adjusting to a less lavish lifestyle, and Nat just couldn't stop trying to meet his daughter's every need. He also couldn't stop being critical of his son-in-law, and soon the situation drifted back to the way it had been before. Nat kept indulging, and Betsy couldn't say no—she had a deep belief that she needed all these material things that only Daddy could provide. A sad divorce followed a year of struggle.

The Early Warning Signs

Although it is often difficult, I urge couples to talk about potential problems that may arise between their two families. It is true that we don't marry a person, we marry a family. We marry traditions, expectations, and psychological mind-sets. We bring our own past into a marriage, too.

Had they been mature and closely bonded, Sue and Sam could have foreseen the difficulty that they were going to have with Cheryl. Both, however, were immature. Sam just wanted peace. Why couldn't these two women just take care of him without all this ruckus? Sue foolishly believed that everything would be blissful with her husband-to-be if Cheryl would just butt out. She failed to understand that the man to whom she was about to commit her life was still a little boy in many ways. And Cheryl believed she owned her children and could set the standard for how they should be treated. She had made decisions for Sam before, and she expected this behavior to continue in the future. If Betsy and Jon had been mature, they would have had some heart-to-heart talks about how they were going to handle Betsy's father. Jon might have said, "You know, I won't be making as much money as your father. We'll have to live more simply, especially when we have children."

Betsy might have said, "I understand that, but I'm used to having what I want. My father has money, so why shouldn't he spend it on me?"

"Well, can we decide together what we'll accept from him? Can we talk about this now and set some limits?"

"Why should we?"

"Because it means a lot to me that we do. Your father has always thought I'm not good enough for you. His gifts might be fine in some ways, but they also send a message that he doesn't think I'm a good enough provider. When you accept them it makes me feel inadequate."

"I hadn't thought of it that way—but I think you're taking this too seriously. You'll benefit from his gifts as well."

"Wait a minute, though. It's not like we're poor. The house we're buying is better than most of our friends could dream about. And we have the money to start a family right away. We're doing very well."

"Are you saying you don't want the furniture he's buying us as a wedding gift? I like that furniture."

"If it's truly a one-time gift, that's fine. But he's already talking about a family vacation in Europe next summer, and he's hinted about buying you a new car for your birthday. I'm concerned that it won't stop—besides, we'll have to pay for the insurance on a car we can't afford. We need to set guidelines."

"I still don't see why. . . ."

Some people might read this exchange and say, "If they'd had that talk, they might not have gotten married!" Or "She's too spoiled, and he's too threatened. They should go to counseling or something." It's possible that if they had seriously discussed the potential difficulties with Nat, Jon might have determined that Betsy was not prepared to break away from her father. He might have decided to postpone the wedding, shocking Betsy into thinking about the issue that was important to him. Or she might have said, "If you feel that way, let's call the wedding off. I don't want to be deprived, and if you're threatened, then so long to you."

From the point of view of a family therapist, I would recommend premarital counseling for a couple in this kind of situation. Jon's mistake was not talking about these issues before the marriage, and he lived to endure the consequences. Betsy had no need to discuss guidelines for her father's generosity. She didn't think his generosity was an issue. She was unable to see that the potential problems were not just about Jon's self-esteem and sense of worthiness but also were intertwined with her inability to separate from her father and his expectations and desire to "make his little girl happy." In this case, Betsy chose to remain a princess. She paid the price of losing her marriage because she didn't want to become a grown woman.

In Sue, Sam, and 's case, the conversation that should have been taking place between the couple was actually going on between the bride and the mother-in-law.

IF YOU are reading this book because you see in-law problems looming in your future, then take a few minutes to determine how the conversations are taking place. Are you talking to your brother or mother about your future spouse's family? Are you complaining to your best friend but not saying anything to your intended? If this is happening, realize that the griping you are doing today is not going to miraculously cease after the wedding. The seeds of unhappiness are being planted now, and the best time to rip them out of the ground is before the marriage vows are exchanged.

I remain convinced that the best way to handle in-law problems is to talk about them as a couple. State your expectations and see if you can work out boundaries agreeable to both of you. Complaining to your siblings or your own parents not only won't solve the problem, it can actually make it worse.

Siblings Are Part of the Baggage, Too

When we discuss in-laws, we usually emphasize parents-in-law. We don't have many "brother-in-law" or "sister-in-law" jokes in our culture, but we certainly could have. Siblings that do nothing but argue and fight can revitalize their loyalties when one of them prepares to marry. Geraldine told me that one of her three future sisters-in-law warned her that she couldn't expect to be welcomed into the family. "We need time to size you up," she said, "and there are no guarantees that we'll think much of you. We've always watched out for Tom, and we'll keep on doing it." Geraldine saw this as a veiled threat—she had to behave in a certain way and measure up to expectations that weren't even defined. I see the statement as an explicit threat, not so veiled as bold.

Fortunately, Geraldine and Tom talked about his sisters

and their strange behavior. Tom might have had several possible reactions. He could have:

* told Geraldine to ignore his sisters and forget the whole thing,

* recounted all his sisters had done for him over the years, especially after their mother died,

* outlined how Geraldine was expected to behave, emphasizing how important it was to him that she make a good impression on his sisters, the only family he has,

* spoken to his sisters and explained that while he appreciated their concern for him, he wasn't going to sit idle while the woman he loved was criticized and threatened.

Fortunately, Tom chose the last option. He called his sister on her behavior and expressed his own hurt feelings. In other words, he took the focus off of his bride-to-be and talked about how he felt. He didn't spend his time defending Geraldine, who didn't need defending.

One of the Guys

Ralph has five brothers, and they have been a team all their lives, even going to the same city college and working at the same summer jobs. Being the first to become engaged, Ralph had a difficult time carving out time for the woman he was marrying in six months. His brothers invited themselves to join the couple for dinner, and they showed up unannounced at Ralph's apartment almost every evening to watch basketball or football games on television. On weekends, they met at the gym to work out. If Ralph didn't show up, they called him and kidded him about oversleeping.

Ralph's girlfriend, Rita, knew the brothers were close, but she hadn't realized how much time they spent together. When Ralph was courting her, they spent time alone. But the minute the engagement ring was on her finger, he changed. Now he was hanging out with his brothers, comfortable being one of guys. But, Rita wanted to know, was it going to be like this after they were married? Well, Ralph said, he did think the boys would be around quite a bit, probably bringing their girlfriends with them from time to time. Ralph admitted that while he loved his brothers, he resented their dropping in unannounced and using his apartment as a gathering place. He acknowledged that he had to set some guidelines, but he was afraid that he'd hurt their feelings, and that terrified him.

Ralph and his brothers sound like the subject of a movie plot. Wedding bells were breaking up that old gang of theirs, and shifting the primary bonds was going to be a painful process. As it turned out, Ralph's brothers did feel rejected when Ralph told them not to come to his house without calling first. He also told them to stop treating Rita like a waitress when they were there. Rita made it clear to Ralph that she was not going to fix their snacks and make sure they had enough beer and soda. These were grown men, after all, and they could wait on themselves.

Compromise, compromise. In this case, it worked. Rita's brother was sometimes included in the sports gatherings, and she and her sister-in-law went to the movies or did other things they wanted to do when the brothers got together. The brothers were hurt, but it had more to do with their reluctance to break away from the past than feeling rejected. Fortunately, these issues were resolved before the wedding. This is good, because I've certainly heard many tales of grief over women who spend all their time with their sisters and men whose brothers become fixtures on the couch. The husbands feel displaced, and the wives often feel ignored, and in some cases, they resent being treated like servants whose job it is to wait on and clean up after the men. Sometimes the individuals balk at changing. After all, they say, my sisters and I have always been close. Or the brothers in this family like to hang out, so why should we change?

Marriage always leads to changes in the family dynamics —it must be so or new family units would never be created. The stories included here offer only a small sampling of the kinds of issues that can surface during the engagement period—or even before. A marriage is a major life change, not just for the couple, but for family and friends as well.

In-law problems don't appear out of the blue; signs of what's to come always exist. Too often, we ignore the issues and tell ourselves that once we're actually married the problems will go away. They don't. This is the time to think logically, even amid the glow of new love.

Sometimes planning the wedding provides the testing ground, so to speak. What can and should be a happy event too often turns into a series of mini-nightmares that offer glimpses into family dynamics we may not have noticed before—and we don't like what we see. The pre-wedding period is the best time for a couple to solidify their own bond and for in-laws to accept a reduced role in a couple's life. In the next chapter, we'll look at this stress-filled time and see how a variety of people handle—or mishandle—this event.

3 JUMPING OVER HURDLES ON THE WAY TO THE ALTAR

*E**ntire*** industries are devoted to planning weddings; we can hire consultants to walk us through every step and each detail, from major to minute. This growing group of consultants helps the engaged couple choose just about everything, from the dresses to the salad dressing to the number of tiers on the cake. Young women who aren't even engaged yet collect the latest issues of brides' magazines. No doubt about it, weddings are the stuff of dreams. Wedding plans often start early in life—some little girls even stage make-believe weddings with their dolls.

Many parents, too, look forward to their child's wedding, expecting that it will be a magnificent event, where they will shine right along with their beloved offspring. For some parents, deciding how to pay for wedding expenses is a decision almost as important as setting up a fund for a college education.

Interesting to note, many young men don't become particularly dreamy about their weddings and generally don't share in the expectant thrill over the event. In our culture, we still prime girls to think of marriage as the beginning of "real" life, but our boys absorb the message that a wedding signals the end of their wild youth and unencumbered lives. For young men, getting married is equal to taking on adult responsibilities. Apprehensive though they may be, young men who are ready for the commitment often find the engagement period an exciting time, too.

So, if weddings are firmly entrenched as a cultural ritual, regardless of ethnicity or religion, what goes wrong? Why do we hear so many nightmarish stories about weddings? And why do in-law relationships become strained, often setting the tone for the early years of marriage, if not for the duration of the relationship—and even beyond divorce or a spouse's death? The answers range from the lofty, involving the complexity of human relationships and genuine difficulties parents may have in letting go of their children, to the out-and-out petty. Weddings often bring out the worst as well as the best in people.

My first experience with planning a wedding, other than my own, was my eldest daughter's wedding, which went well for the most part. We had a few rough moments and some disagreements, but all in all, the memories are pleasant. My daughter, Faith, and I remember a few amusing incidents, one of which took place in the bridal shop where we were looking at wedding dresses. The talkative and friendly saleswoman warned us about problems that might arise as we went about making the plans. It seems that the saleswoman's mother-in-law had driven her crazy during the time she was planning her wedding and then for months afterward. One altercation after another set the tone, particularly when this woman's future mother-in-law informed her about the "right" way to do things. Finally, after Faith and I had an earful of these stories, I asked the woman how she and her mother-in-law got along now. "Oh," she said, "we have the ideal relationship—we don't speak to each other." This story isn't as rare as we'd like to think!

Many Cooks in the Stew of Choices

When we anticipate planning a wedding, we think of lovely days of shopping and choosing the location of the wedding and going over the guest list for the reception. We tend to think of the exciting choices involved in planning the color scheme or choosing the band, if music and dancing will be part of the event. To be sure, a wedding is a major undertaking, but in some families, anyway, the event has been anticipated for years.

With all the choices to be made, it's no wonder that every member of the family has an opinion. Ideally, the bride and the groom have agreed on the size and scope of the wedding, and the choices are narrowed. They announce what they are planning, and everyone falls in line to support them. Unfortunately, as we'll see, harmony isn't always easily achieved. Much of the time, old family issues, conflicting feelings about the marriage, and other assorted jealousies and disagreements interfere. Many of these difficulties are eventually resolved, but some are not, and unfortunately, they're hauled into the marriage like a bag of garbage that weighs everyone down.

I firmly believe in learning from others' experiences. If you're planning a wedding and already have problems, perhaps you can gain insight from other people's experiences. Let's look at a few scenarios and see how problems were—or weren't—resolved.

The Rose-Colored Dress

Lucy is one of my best friends, and I had watched her daughter, Rachel, develop from an adorable infant into a lovely young woman. Now she was about to be married. Since I had always been very close to Rachel, I was thrilled to be included in the wedding plans. I was involved in the discussions about bridesmaid's dresses with Rachel and Lucy, and we knew exactly what we were looking for. The three of us love to shop, so we thought getting together with the bridesmaids to look for the dresses was going to be fun for all of us.

Rachel explained to the bridesmaids, including two sisters-in-law-to-be, what she had in mind. The fun ended just about that time. One sister-in-law explained that she could wear only a dress with straight lines because she was a bit overweight, and the other sister-in-law said she could never wear rose because it made her look pale and sickly. As it turned out, they had their own ideas about what they should wear.

Rachel was willing to make some compromises, so at first we thought these differences could be resolved. But the two young women wanted what they wanted and were quite inflexible. Days of shopping turned into weeks of bickering, as other family members put in their two cents worth about the dress dilemma. Before long, the wedding plans were poisoned with angry accusations and hurt feelings as the families took sides about the style and color of the dresses.

The groom's mother became involved, insisting that her daughters had a right to select what they wanted, especially since they were paying for the dresses. It was a special day for the bridesmaids, too, she insisted. Their only brother was getting married, and they should have a say. Rachel's father is a lovely, sweet-tempered man who said that none of it mattered anyway, and the young women should wear what suited them. Lucy said that it was up to Rachel—she was the bride. I, too, couldn't resist voicing my opinion, so I declared that it was all up to the bride, period, end of story.

Eventually, attempts to be polite about the conflict broke

down, and the anger turned to silence for a time, followed by screaming and yelling. Rachel is usually even-tempered, but she became cranky, and Lucy was an emotional wreck. The groom became involved and felt very much caught in the middle, although he tried to restore peace. Poor guy, his efforts made Rachel angry at him, too! Finally, the tension boiled over, and Rachel screamed at her future in-laws, informing them that she never wanted to see them again in her life and that the wedding was off. Naturally, the in-law family had some ugly words of their own to share. As the groom likes to describe it, all parties "sounded like raving idiots."

Whew! Somehow, rose-colored dresses were purchased, although not in the style Rachel wanted, and Rachel and her groom had their wedding after all. The relatives in both families were cordial, but underneath the calm, the sisters-in-law seethed, and Rachel continued to believe that she'd been treated badly. While the wedding day was still quite nice, the tension had taken its toll, and Rachel's "big day" didn't live up to her expectations.

Even worse, the relationship between Rachel and her in-law family was off to a terrible start. Sadly, it has never recovered. For her husband's sake, Rachel sees her sisters-in-law, but she admits that she will always be angry at them for ruining her wedding day.

Most people hear these stories and have one of three reactions:

* They wonder how intelligent people could have let such petty issues overwhelm them and ruin budding relationships—surely, they think, an amicable solution could have been found.

* They identify with the sisters-in-law and think about their own bad experiences—they might begin telling wedding stories of their own.

✳ They identify with the bride and talk about the nerve of that in-law family trying to run things. The story brings back personal resentments that have never quite gone away.

Perhaps there's a fourth reaction—These people need to manage their stress better! But in truth, as stressful as wedding preparations can be, stress alone can't be blamed for all the problems. The real issues are concealed as the family fights over tiny details. In other words, it looks like stress, but deeper concerns are involved, and wedding plans trigger unspoken problems.

Ambivalent Feelings Equal Ambivalent Wedding Plans

Smooth or rocky wedding plans often depend on the way families feel about the impending marriage. One family I know described the son's fiancée as a "stranger," a woman lurking about waiting to carry out her plan to rob the family of the love and attention that was rightfully theirs. This sounds radical, indeed, and not all feelings might be as clear or as extreme, but often enough, negative attitudes toward the bride or groom come out in statements like, "She's going to have the reception in that tacky hotel?" or "You mean that bum of a brother is going to be his best man?" or "What kind of stupid cake is that?"

In Rachel's case, it could be that the color of the bridesmaid's dresses wasn't the issue at all. It's possible that the other girls were envious or jealous of the bride, resentful that she was taking a very indulgent brother away from them. The girls were used to getting what they wanted from and being pampered by their brother. They adored him, but since meeting Rachel, he didn't spend as much time with them. Under the guise of a disagreement over a dress, they were coping with unfamiliar feelings of loss, jealousy, and even perhaps a sense of betrayal.

If you find yourself enmeshed in a squabble that seems so ridiculous that you can't begin to understand why it's happening, consider that the crisis at hand may not be the issue that's causing the emotional eruptions. It could be something much deeper being acted out on a stage called a wedding.

If we state one goal for a wedding, perhaps it should be that the families remain intact after it's over! Perhaps that should be part of our dreams as we fantasize about the perfect wedding. But, as we'll see, reaching that goal may be next to impossible in some situations, and we have to make the best of the cards we're dealt.

Where's Mamma?

Irene had an image in her mind about the perfect woman for her only son, Stan. The woman would be young and beautiful and eager to have many children. Irene wanted nothing more than to become a grandmother. Her dreams were shattered when she met Leslie, Stan's fiancée, a woman ten years older than Stan, with two teenagers—all these facts were nails in the coffin, so to speak. Worst of all, babies were not part of the couple's future plans.

After hours and days and months of trying to talk her son out of marrying "that woman," other family members and friends had had enough. Her husband and the rest of the family started pleading with her to make the best of it and accept Stan's choice. For a while it looked as if reason had returned, and Irene was quiet about her concerns.

How wrong the family was. Without telling anyone, Irene came up with a drastic plan. She'd buy off the bride! It had worked in a movie she'd seen, and she'd seen it happen in television soaps too. Surely, Leslie would accept a very large sum of money in return for ending the engagement. To add insult to injury, she called Leslie's family, told them about the bribe she was offering, and tried to enlist their support in persuading the woman to accept the terms. Leslie's family thought it was a joke, but Leslie was horrified, and of course, she told Stan. Humiliated and shocked, Stan was even more amazed when his mother threatened to disinherit him if he went ahead with the wedding. Confrontation simply didn't work with Irene. When Stan told her that he was marrying Leslie no matter what, Irene then said she wouldn't attend the wedding, nor would she speak to him again. Irene had worked up such a head of steam over this that she couldn't back down. This situation is extreme, but sadly, it is a true story. Things like this do happen.

Gradually, Irene began to relent a little, and she announced that she would come to the wedding. She arrived at the church at the appointed time, but she wouldn't go in. She sat in the car and said she'd appear at the reception. No one saw her there either, and everyone was so disgusted —even her husband—that no one bothered to look for her. When the reception ended, Irene came out of the ladies' room, where she had been hiding out for several hours.

Before this happened, no one would have believed Irene was capable of such awful behavior. Known to be kind, thoughtful, and considerate, Irene shocked her family and friends. They had no choice but to conclude that she had truly "gone crazy" when she couldn't have the one thing in life she apparently wanted more than anything else, her own grandchildren.

I have followed this family's story for many years, and I regret that Irene hasn't yet come to terms with Leslie and Stan's marriage. She is convinced that Stan has wronged her and that he should have considered *her* wishes when he chose a wife. She wanted grandchildren, and now her dream is lost. Although Stan and Leslie continue to invite her to family gatherings, she sulks when she does appear, behavior that is beginning to wear on the couple. It's a tragic situation because Irene is in danger of losing her son, along with the dream of grandchildren.

Most parents probably fantasize about the day they will become grandparents. It's a natural desire. However, we don't give birth to our children for the purpose of being "given" grandchildren. What would Irene have done if her son had married a younger woman, but they were unable to have children? What if Stan and a different bride had decided not to have children? Who would she have blamed? Would she still have lost all reason? What if Stan and a bride adopted their children? Would she have been one of those (fortunately) rare grandparents who wouldn't have accepted a child not genetically related to her? We'll never know, but until the situation arose, no one, not even her husband, had any idea how deep Irene's desire for grandchildren was. In this case, and others like it, I recommend counseling, sometimes for the couple, but most certainly for the parent whose reactions are out of control.

At times the concern over a child's choice of a spouse are legitimate, and trying to reason with the son or daughter makes sense. No one wants to see a child marry a drug addict or a person with a serious criminal past. I've seen parents wring their hands over a child's marriage to a person who couldn't hold a job, and, furthermore, didn't intend to try. These are heartbreaking situations, and often parents must grieve over the choice, accept it, do the best they can at the wedding, and then move on. If the child is an adult, the parents really have no other choice except totally alienating themselves from their child.

Much of the time, however, the hysterics that go on,

while not as extreme as Irene's reaction, are over something far less important. I know Leslie, and she's a hardworking, attractive woman who has raised two lovely kids on her own. Not a thing is wrong with her. Everyone else knew this, but Irene remains unable to listen to reason.

If you are in a similar situation, even if not as extreme, what should you do? I recommend the following:

1. **The couple should be very clear with each other about the situation and talk it through honestly.** What if Leslie hadn't told Stan about Irene's bribe? Most family secrets see the light of day eventually, and Stan might have felt betrayed if Leslie had kept the secret, even if she said she remained quiet to spare his feelings. (Since Irene got her idea from movies and soaps, she should have known that the "secret" is always revealed.)

2. **The couple should make every attempt to separate what affects them as a couple from what doesn't.** Irene's behavior didn't adversely affect Stan's relationship with his step-children, nor did it affect their choice of a home or their honeymoon plans. They had to work around Irene when making wedding plans, because they weren't sure if she would cause a scene. Stan talked with his father, who was terribly upset over his wife's behavior, about this potential problem. Enlisting his father's cooperation and support was a wise move.

3. **The couple should do their best to understand the troublesome person or people if they can.** When a parent is behaving as badly as Irene, we must assume that psychological issues are surfacing and that perhaps the person is in emotional trouble.

4. **Assuming the situation isn't as extreme as Leslie and Stan's, try to keep a sense of humor.** Remember that the

bond with the spouse-to-be is the most important one to protect, and in many cases, these pre-wedding problems do smooth out over time. Sometimes humor can ease tensions when reason and logic can't.

5. **If possible, talk about the disagreements openly and honestly with other family members.** Concealing dislike often leads to pressures that eventually surface and cause permanent rifts in the family.

Dislike of a new in-law is one reason arguments start during the pre-wedding period, but it is certainly not the only cause. Sometimes the reasons weddings become battlegrounds hit much closer to home.

I'll Walk Alone

As a little girl, Jill dreamed about the dramatic walk down the aisle with her beloved daddy. But when it was time to plan her wedding, she hadn't seen her father, Bill, in two years. He was living on the opposite coast with his new, third wife. Still, Jill knew what she wanted, and when she asked him to "give her away" at the wedding, he eagerly accepted the honor.

Sounds simple, but this one act ignited the fires of rage. Jill's mother, Rhonda, was furious because Jill hadn't asked her stepfather, Craig, to walk her down the aisle. After all, he'd been more of a father to her than her real father. Kind and gentle, he'd provided for her since she was nine years old and had seen her through some tough times. Besides, he was paying for most of the wedding.

The battle raged between mother and daughter. Everyone in the family had an opinion, and the arguments escalated. Just when everyone thought the situation couldn't get worse, Jill told her mother that her dad had asked if he could bring his new wife to the wedding, and not wanting to hurt his feelings, she'd said yes. This was enough to make Rhonda threaten to boycott the wedding.

Jill ended up walking down the aisle alone, not an uncommon practice today, giving both "dads" special seats in the front row. The new wife came, but Rhonda tried to ensure that no one would talk to her. This situation is complex because each person has a "story," a version of what happened in the past and what should happen now. These are the stories:

—*Rhonda had been badly wounded when Jill's father left her for a younger woman. Even though she was happily remarried, the devastation and heartbreak of that long-ago period in her life hadn't completely healed. She still entertained revenge fantasies from time to time. (She must have been thrilled when the second marriage broke up.)*

—*Craig loved Jill and had treated her like his own daughter. He was bound to feel some pangs at the thought that the "no-goodnick" father and first husband was going to suddenly appear on the scene and play the "daddy" role.*

—*Bill had maintained a relationship with Jill, even if he wasn't always as close to her as her stepfather.*

—*Jill's fiancé, Joe, and his family have a part in this story, too. They stayed completely out of it. Joe told Jill that whatever she decided was okay with him, and he never raised the subject with Rhonda.*

—*Jill loved both fathers in her life. She didn't want to hurt either of them, but she still thought that her "real" father should be given the honor of walking her down the aisle.*

Jill and her mother were able to work out their difficulties because they had been close all their lives. Jill's bond to her mother was stronger than her tie to her biological father, and she wasn't willing to deeply hurt her mother. Rhonda was able to back off and tell Jill she'd been wrong to be so angry about Bill's role in the wedding. Both were willing to compromise, and the two women felt bad that they had hurt each other. In this case, it just happened to be Jill who gave in and altered her plan.

This resolution would not necessarily work for everyone. Some might argue that weddings are no place to resolve old issues and that the bride should have exactly what she wants. I usually take this position, but in this case, the ability to talk about the conflict led to an agreement that worked out fairly well. Jill learned that sometimes a principle isn't as important as how someone we love feels. The two dads were each a bit hurt, but we could say that it was an equal opportunity hurt—neither walked their daughter down the aisle, so neither was considered more important than the other in the wedding. Thankfully, Jill's in-laws and her groom kept their opinions to themselves and didn't get involved in an issue they had no part in. Can you imagine what might have happened if Joe or his family had tried to "help"?

So-and-So Had Better Not Show Up

Like Rhonda, many people don't welcome seeing an ex-mate with a new partner at a child's wedding. However, with the divorce and remarriage rate we have in our culture, this situation will become more common, not less. No single solution works for everyone, so we can't come up with a set of guidelines that will work every time. However, if you're the person who has threatened not to attend a wedding if so-and-so will be there, stop and think about whose day this actually is. Will you really die if a person you despise is invited to the wedding? Short of that, will your life truly be ruined? Will you *never get over it?*

One of the most revealing events for the two families is the task of making out the guest lists and seating arrangements for the wedding. In some cases, it can take hours, because Aunt Josie can't be seated at the same table as her ex-husband, and Uncle Abel isn't bringing a date, so he has to be placed far away from his ex-wife, who is bringing her much younger lover. The parents of the bride have to separate their parents because the two sets of in-laws haven't spoken for thirty years. Nothing complicated here. All this is made more difficult if various members of the family make demands about with whom they will or will not sit.

Most of us wrongly assume that age usually leads to greater wisdom, but as a therapist, some of the craziest situations I've ever seen occurred in families whose older members need to grow up or they'll hurt the very young people they claim to love.

Don't Bring the Stranger

After Bert's wife died, he was lonely and celibate for many years. Then, at sixty-nine, he met Milly. He adores her, and they've lived together for five years, but don't plan to marry. Bert has told his sisters that his second chance at love has made him the happiest man alive.

Bert's sisters, now in their seventies and eighties, were very fond of his first wife and were disappointed when he "took up" with *her.* All three sisters are widowed, and before Milly came along, they liked pampering Bert and spending time with him. The sisters and other family members often have big gatherings with all the children and grandchildren attending. The sisters reluctantly include Milly, but she's not accepted as part of the family. Bernice, the oldest sister, believes Bert is being "unfaithful" to his late wife and gossips about the way he is "carrying on like a teenager."

Bernice's granddaughter announced her wedding plans, which included her Uncle Bert and Milly. But Bernice would have none of it and said, "Bert, you can't bring a stranger to the wedding."

For his part, Bert knew how his sisters felt about Milly and generally ignored them, but this was too much. He told his sisters he was through with the lot of them, and bitter arguments ensued. The young bride saved the day, obviously having more sense than her grandmother. Milly was included, Bernice didn't like it, and the bride ignored the whole thing, except to joke with her friends about the description of her Uncle Bert's much-loved friend as a "stranger." She and her friends had a good laugh, and this young bride now has a funny story to tell about her silly relatives.

So, is this what we want? When other family members talk about us years from now, do we want to be the main character in a story, especially one where we either disrupted a wedding or posed a potential threat of doing so? When we take the long view, most of us would rather be thought of as the peacemakers, not the peace breakers. Bad enough we should get a reputation as a difficult mother-in-law, but who wants to be known as the hurtful aunt or busybody grandmother? Perhaps we'd have less trouble blending families if we took a mental trip fifteen or twenty-five years into the future and retold the tale.

Problems with wedding plans have probably been with us since the days when we all ate roots and berries in the hosting family's cave. As larger clans and societies developed, nuptial customs, rituals, and rules were created, too. We made rules about where the bride and groom will live after the ceremony, whose family is dominant in the couple's lives, and how the engagement should be handled in the first place. In some cultures, including many who make up the mixture of societies that blend in our country, marriages were arranged, and the bride and groom never had a chance to disagree about the wedding since they didn't even know each other.

Sometimes modern engagements and weddings, not to mention all the complicated family relationships, make us long for the good ol' days, when our customs might have been restrictive, but we all knew what they were. Now we have a potpourri of ideas and traditions, and no one is quite sure what the rules are. If we're honest, most of us admit that we like it better this newer way. But when big events like weddings take place, we may feel somewhat lost because we don't know what to do without a set of guidelines. Given our varying ideas about these cultural events, it is especially important that we tread carefully over unknown ground. Many in-law problems develop because of fundamental misunderstandings about the "right" way to do things.

Who's Paying for This Shindig Anyway?

In this country, it's traditional for the bride's parents to pay most of the expenses for their daughter's wedding. That was a nearly universal standard adhered to by most people. But our culture has changed, and now it is common for the groom's family to make a financial contribution as well. Or, in some situations, the bride and groom—who may be well along in their careers and perhaps better off financially than their parents—pay their own bills and plan the wedding without much family involvement.

The time to straighten out the financial arrangements is when the wedding plans begin. In most situations, it is reasonable to assume that paying for something means having a role in determining how the money is spent. However, when we plan a wedding, this assumption can and does create problems, and sometimes two sets of in-laws become involved.

I believe that if the parents pay for the wedding, it should be viewed as a gift, unless otherwise specified. Giving a gift usually means "no strings attached." The couple chooses what they want, and the wedding decisions are in their hands. In most cases, they listen to their families, consider their suggestions, and may even like some of them! Ultimately, though, the final decisions rest with the couple. I believe this is a good rule of thumb. So, what happens when a couple knows what they want but don't manage to get it? Lessons can be learned from a couple who couldn't say no.

Let's Keep It Simple

Kate and Ed agreed on every detail of their wedding. A small ceremony in a neighborhood church, followed by an Italian buffet, complete with a variety of pastas and wine in the party room of a nearby restaurant—one of the bride and groom's favorite haunts. Music would be provided by a three-piece band the couple had recently discovered and enjoyed. They congratulated themselves on planning a simple wedding, but one that was ideal for them.

The wedding that actually took place was held in the Crystal Champagne Room, one of the most expensive banquet halls in their city. The ceremony was followed by a buffet cocktail party that preceded a five-course dinner. The seven-piece band played until the wee hours of the morning, while the guests, dressed in black tie, danced, drank champagne, and helped themselves to Viennese treats from the dessert table.

What an event! It cost a fortune, but who cares? Everyone said it was a great wedding. Even Kate and Ed always say they had a great time. Alone, away from their families, they will also admit they were disappointed that their wedding wasn't the small, simple one they had agreed on.

So, what happened? How did they get from the neighborhood church to the champagne boulevard? Kate and Ed couldn't stick to their choices. They became trapped in their parents' dreams of splendor and gave up their own dream of intimacy and close friends dancing to the little band. Unable to hurt their parents' feelings, they ended up with their parents' fantasies, not their own. Something is wrong with this picture. Kate and Ed still feel odd about the money that was spent on their wedding, money that neither family could afford. No arguments actually took place here, but Kate and Ed didn't get what they wanted.

Both Kate and Ed are slightly resentful about the domineering attitudes of both families. While this isn't serious, the family relationships are subtly strained. If Kate and Ed were to say anything, they'd be accused of being ungrateful children. What could those kids be thinking? Their parents spent *thousands!* If they don't say anything, they'll feel misunderstood and discounted. After all, whose wedding was it supposed to be? Fortunately, Kate and Ed learned a lesson from their experience. When other big events occur, such as buying a home and having a family, they are forewarned about the interference that could take place. Together, they have resolved to stand up to their parents and stick to their own choices.

I could provide one hundred pages of tips for avoiding conflict, and that still wouldn't be enough. Problems do occur, and sometimes they seem unavoidable. Still, we can follow a few basic guidelines designed to head off serious wedding-plan problems that can lead to permanent rifts in a family or even temporary ugliness that no one wants to remember years later.

Use these guidelines as general suggestions, ideas that

should help keep peace in the family if they're explained clearly.

For the couple:

1. **It's your wedding, so do it your way.** If you want a traditional wedding, fine; if you don't, then others might try to convince you that only one way is "right." Whatever you do, someone will find a reason to be critical, so follow your own heart and have the wedding you want within the agreed-upon financial limits.

2. **Invite the people with whom you want to share your special day.** If others threaten not to come, let them make their own choices.

3. **Children love weddings, and if you want them included, invite them.** If you prefer a more "dignified" affair, politely and firmly tell parents that this is an adults-only wedding. Expect some people to be angry.

4. **When in doubt, don't leave people out.** Many people want to invite everyone and plan a more simple wedding in order to have a large event. Some people who plan an expensive affair later regret that they left certain people, even relatives, off the guest list because of the expense. They wish they'd had a less lavish wedding, but with more people attending.

5. **Discuss finances ahead of time with those paying for the wedding.** If the bride's family is paying, find out what the guidelines are and don't overstep them. I've seen too many people go deeply into debt because they wanted to have the "best" wedding. But some of the best weddings don't cost very much. If you're paying for the wedding, with perhaps a little help from your families, then be sure you agree on the scope of the event. This is an opportunity to have what you want, but don't plan

a wedding that you can't pay for without hardship. If the wedding is a three-way event, the same guidelines apply. Plan what you want within the budget that these joint circumstances allow.

6. **Don't seat "enemies" together, but don't go crazy trying to please everyone.** Some people will be unhappy no matter where you seat them. A woman I know actually left a wedding because she was seated with the bride's family's maid and her husband. I say, let her leave. Who needs this kind of guest anyway?

7. **Spend as much (within your budget) or as little as you want.** No matter what you do, someone will criticize your choices. If your wedding is lavish, people will say you're ostentatious and tacky. If you have a simple wedding, people will say you—or your families—are cheap.

8. **Attempt to talk with family members who are critical of your plans.** Listen to them and try to understand their feelings. Please them if you can, but don't give in to wedding plans that make you unhappy.

9. **Consider a small intimate wedding.** Sometimes a big wedding triggers too many problems. A small affair with immediate family and close friends can be memorable and lovely. Small weddings may be preferable if many family conflicts and tensions exist. But don't go small if you've always dreamed about a big wedding. Consider a small wedding as an option only if, as a couple, it will make you happy.

10. **Stick together; I can't emphasize this enough.** This is not the time to have a knee-jerk reaction and side with your family members. If your sister hurt the groom's feelings, then acknowledge that. If your father is nasty to your future wife, then speak up. If you make decisions about what is best for the two of you, you will

have taken a big step toward avoiding future family arguments. Most in-law problems would not develop if the couple agreed about the way to deal with their families.

11. **You make the decisions; you take the consequences.** Count on some people being angry over your choices. You can't please everyone, so on this big day, please yourself.

For the parents:

1. **State your budget and stick to it.** Decide what you can afford and tell the couple you plan to maintain the boundaries. Don't put yourself in financial jeopardy. This is your right. Nowadays, your children may have been out on their own for several years before they marry, and some prefer to pay for their own wedding. Either way, state what you can do and hold firm.

2. **Voice your preferences and suggestions.** You are entitled to hope that the children will like your ideas. If they don't, then forget it. This is their wedding, not yours. If your own wedding wasn't exactly as you wanted it, you shouldn't recreate an ideal wedding and impose it on your kids.

3. **Put your own family feuds aside.** Barring some extreme situation, your ex-spouse and former in-laws have a right to be at your child's wedding. Sniping about relatives or ex-relatives you don't care for builds tension and causes incredible stress for your children.

4. **Honor your children's plans, give them your blessing, enjoy yourself, and let them do it their way.** Have a good time no matter what.

Wedding Rules Are Meant to Be Broken—
If You Choose To

If we don't enjoy being part of another culture's rituals, even if for only a day, we are jaded indeed. If we're lucky, we'll be invited to many weddings, and perhaps participate in them too, where everything that is done seems different. Perhaps the ceremony will take place on a beach or the flowers will be picked from the groom's garden. Gospel choirs will blend with Israeli folk music or Greek dancing will follow a Vietnamese wedding blessing. Nowadays, ministers and rabbis officiate together, and when done well, the guests, at least those who care about these things, think it was the best Christian wedding or the best Jewish wedding they've ever seen, depending on their point of view.

People who maintain an open mind usually have a great time at these bashes. A friend of mine tells the story about the maid of honor who showed up at the wedding sporting body tattoos and a nose ring, shocking the bride's future in-laws. But by the end of the day, the new in-laws thought this young woman, a brilliant artist, was just terrific—an original to be sure, but then, so was the bride, and they were crazy about her.

In recent years, unconventional weddings have become almost the norm, and many are just wonderful. One of the loveliest and most meaningful weddings I've attended recently took place in the garden of a beautiful old mansion. The simple ceremony was written by the bride and groom, so it was personally meaningful. Another took place on a beautiful moonlit beach, and still another was held in the small house that the bride and groom had lived in for two years. In each case, the bride and groom planned their unique wedding without criticism from relatives. They didn't hear anyone say, "I'll *die* if you do that" or "Your grandmother will be *devastated* if you invite so-and-so." Perhaps the only rule followed in these weddings was that everyone remembered whose wedding it was.

Ties Are Broken, Ties Are Mended

We all have stories in our families about weddings that created a rough spot in the life cycle of the in-law relationship. Happily, many of these situations are resolved once the wedding is over, and life goes back to normal. If resolution doesn't happen immediately, then sometimes the birth of a child or another life event repairs the bonds.

If a couple discovers, however, that the wounds aren't healing, then they can find themselves in trouble as they attempt to appease all the people they love. Even worse, their own conflicts intensify if they weigh loyalty to each other against loyalty to their families. During the early years of marriage, many couples try to restructure family ties. In the next chapter, we'll see where the rough spots are likely to occur and how people can cope with them. We'll also explore the consequences of not addressing problems as they arise.

4 SO THE HONEYMOON IS OVER

In-law problems often sound amusing, unless we happen to be in the midst of our own difficulties, in which case they make us wish we'd never met so-and-so in the first place and most certainly not been foolish enough to marry into *that* family. These feelings often begin early in a marriage—the honeymoon glow can dim soon after life is supposedly back to normal. So often, the same annoying issues that caused tension during the engagement period pop up again, usually after a short reprieve that follows the wedding and honeymoon.

A woman I know told me her in-law problems were over the minute she and her new husband left the reception. "How did you manage that?" I asked. "Well," she said, "we had our honeymoon in England, where we continued our studies for two years, and then when we finished there, we left for Africa, where we spent two years on an international service project. By the time we came back to the States, everyone had forgotten all about the trivia that had caused such anguish. Our families were happy to see us come back and start what they considered a normal life, so the fighting stopped. I wish every couple could have a four-year honeymoon."

Indeed! My friend's story makes me envious. Just imagine how blissful their four years alone must have been, despite being so far from the familiar comforts of home. Most of us, however, must face family issues much sooner than this traveling duo. And the early years can be very fragile in a marriage, even when the bride and groom have known each other for years and perhaps even lived together before marrying.

During the early years, in-law tensions can run high, too, especially if expectations haven't been discussed. Too often, we say to ourselves and maybe to our spouse, "Oh well, it will all work itself out." But the fact is, things usually don't work themselves out. We must take action, even when we risk rocking the boat.

From what I see in my practice, in-law problems in the early years of marriage often revolve around issues of how much time the couple will spend with their families, how much "advice" (some people might justifiably call it interference) they'll accept, and even mundane decisions about where they will spend holidays. (In many families, however, these are hardly mundane decisions.)

Mothers-in-law have been the target of the most cruel jokes, but our culture has changed, and it is no longer "politically correct" to single them out as the object of all in-law remarks. In fact, nowadays we often make jokes about the old jokes, happy to have moved on from an era when it was open season on mothers-in-law.

In the past, people often assumed that a mother-in-law, particularly the groom's mother, would constantly criticize her daughter-in-law and meddle in the couple's affairs. And many old stories target the bride's mother, too, often with men joking about schemes to get rid of the "old bag." Some mothers-in-law seem to fall right into the stereotypical patterns. But as we all know, problems with fathers-in-law, siblings-in-law, and even grandparents-in-law are common, too.

Wishful Thinking Doesn't Solve Problems

I'm no longer surprised at how serious in-law problems are for families and individuals. From nagging discontent to full-bodied rage, the range of emotions individuals experience is wide and deep. I've even seen situations in which problems over in-laws led to abusive behavior or a long-lasting depression. I can't help but be puzzled at times. Why would a couple be willing to risk permanent damage to their own relationship rather than joining forces to solve the problem? In other words, why don't more couples do whatever it takes to make their relationship primary? If that means limiting time with in-law families, then so be it. More often, though, I see couples allowing their marriage to be overwhelmed by in-law difficulties. They simply hope the tensions will eventually go away.

Equally disturbing is the fact that otherwise kind, considerate people can become mean-spirited and stubborn—or worse—when they become in-laws. Some years ago, Joyce, a mother-in-law, started singing the praises of one of her son's former girlfriends. Oh, how that girl could cook. And smart? Vivian had a master's degree by the time she was twenty-four. Pretty? No other girl her boy had brought around was as beautiful as that Vivian. And this wonder woman's crowning achievement? Vivian could wrap presents so beautifully that people were reluctant to open them. If this sounds ridiculous, but harmless, let me tell you that

Joyce went on and on about her son's one-time girlfriend during the family Christmas gatherings. After four years of this, Joyce's son finally told her to be quiet about Vivian.

You might think I heard this story in a therapy session with the couple. But that's not the case. Joyce told me the story as a joke on herself. She couldn't believe her own behavior. "It's true," she said, "that I liked Vivian. But I like Eva too. I don't know what got into me. I apologized to Eva after that last Christmas, and she laughed it off. But I bet she tells that story now and then—and I don't blame her. I'd tell it, too, if I were in Eva's position."

At least in this case, Joyce had the good sense to stop a behavior that was at best hurtful and at worst destructive. I also applaud her son for stepping in and insisting she be quiet. As I've said before, in-law problems are always exacerbated if the new partners don't set boundaries and talk to their parents about difficulties.

While studying the life cycle of in-law relationships, I began to reflect on my own experiences. When I first met my future in-laws I had great hopes for the relationship. My relationship with my own parents had been lacking in many ways, and I even had fantasies about my in-laws becoming the parents I had always wanted. Well, that certainly didn't happen. Now, I look back over thirty years of marriage, and I can see friction, frustration, and discontent for all involved because difficulties weren't resolved. We swept them under the rug, and we all hoped they would just go away one day.

I don't mean to imply that in-law relationships are never satisfying. Some in-laws form warm, intimate ties with the new relatives. A few people have told me that they were enriched by new family members and cherished these relationships. We should all look at the successful relationships as role models. What attitudes do the people involved have or what behaviors or "policies" did they adopt that we can learn from? Did they work for these relationships or did they just happen?

Pete, a new father-in-law, told me that he had initially disliked his daughter's husband, Josh, and had been polite but not particularly friendly to him or his family. About six months after the wedding, the new couple invited both families to a Sunday afternoon barbecue.

"This wasn't our first visit to their home," Pete said, "but for some reason, I noticed how nicely Josh was treating my daughter and how he looked at her with such love in his eyes. It was a like a brick hitting me in the head and waking me up. How could I continue to dislike this young man, who has a good education, a good job, and an outgoing personality, just because he has a shaved head and talks like a poet? My daughter reminded me that Josh *is* a poet!"

Fortunately, Pete began treating his son-in-law more like a friend, and by the time grandchildren came along, they had built a trusting relationship. Now Pete raves about what a great father Josh is. For this caring dad, the change in attitude came when he realized not just that his daughter loved Josh, but that Josh loved her, too. Like Joyce, he was able to examine his ambivalence—and his behavior—and change. In-law children have told me similar stories. Sometimes they just stood back from the situation and tried to look at things from the in-law parent's viewpoint. When they did, they resolved the problem internally, that is, they worked on it as their personal problem, not as something that necessarily needed to be worked out with another person. They were also big enough people to admit being wrong.

At times, however, problems are so severe that family and in-law relationships threaten everyone's happiness. It isn't a matter of a simple shift in attitude. Some of the issues I'm illustrating here are often so serious that you may not want or be able to handle them alone. On the surface, they might seem trivial, but if left unresolved, the only way to end them is with a divorce decree.

Everyone Has a Viewpoint

PERHAPS **you've heard the story** about two old friends, Libby and Sara, who run into each other at the mall. Libby asks Sara how her daughter is since her wedding. "Oh," Sara says, "she's just great. She lives in a huge house, has live-in help, two beautiful fur coats, and lots of diamond jewelry. And what about your son and daughter-in-law? How are they doing?"

"That witch," Libby says, "is driving my son to an early grave. He has to work night and day because she wants a bigger house, a live-in maid, diamonds, and a fur coat!"

The same situation can look so different, depending on which side of the fence we're sitting on. The grass doesn't always look greener on the other side, it sometimes looks like a different species of grass. Ed and Lynne were in this situation when they came to counseling. They had been arguing about Ed's mother, Sandra, for seven years. According to Lynne, Ed took his mother's side in absolutely everything, even after she'd done something hurtful to Lynne. Their fighting had escalated, and Lynne was afraid of losing control. For example, just a week before their first counseling session Lynne had became so enraged that she threw Ed's dinner at him—lamb chops, potatoes, and salad. And she proceeded to break some other dishes, too, which shocked her because she loved their handmade pottery plates and bowls.

Lynne described herself as a fairly calm person—easy-going, actually. But her dealings with her mother-in-law were another story. Sandra had been criticizing her from the first day they met. In fact, Lynne told me that her mother-in-law had even told her that she didn't wrap the trash properly and was killing Ed with unhealthy food.

Ed, who'd said very little thus far, admitted that his mother didn't like Lynne, but she hadn't liked any woman he'd dated. Before he'd met Lynne, he'd broken off other relationships because his mother disapproved of them. Reluctantly, Ed agreed that perhaps his mother was unusually jealous.

During several months of counseling, Ed talked at length about his relationship with his mother. She'd been widowed young, and as a single parent, she had worked hard to provide for him. Ed loved his mother deeply and was extremely grateful for all she had done to provide a good life for him. Because she had sacrificed for him, he was reluctant to criticize her for anything. He understood his mother's jealousy, because he had been the center of her world for many years. She was also the center of his, of course, and that was one of the problems.

It took several weeks before Ed could admit that he believed Lynne was partially responsible for his mother's behavior. She didn't take care of him the way his mother had, so, he concluded, why wouldn't his mother criticize?

This was a "make or break" point for this couple. Lynne was furious and deeply hurt. She could have walked away from the marriage, grateful to be away from Sandra and her spoiled son. But she chose to stick with the counseling to see if Ed could grow into the role of a mature husband.

Ed and Lynne were painfully honest with each other, and when Ed acknowledged resenting Lynne because she wasn't more like his mother, it was a positive sign. He had gained insight into his past and was able to admit he had difficulty accepting his role as a husband. His mother had granted his every wish, and he had had no experience with the give-and-take of an adult marriage relationship.

As a definitive step toward resolution, Ed no longer allowed his mother to criticize Lynne. Once Sandra realized that Ed was angry about the way she treated Lynne, she began to back off. Lynne and Ed kept on communicating their feelings as honestly as possible and agreed to be supportive of each other's opinions, even when they didn't agree. Ed remained a loyal son, but he also began growing into a mature man, capable of being a real husband. Lynne came to a deeper understanding of her husband's upbringing and why he would always feel especially close to his mother and genuinely grateful for the sacrifices she'd made for him.

Sandra's criticism was out in the open, and insulting though it was, Ed heard it with his own ears and couldn't deny that it happened.

Let Me Help Out

Teri's in-laws, Ethyl and Ralph, seemed quite pleasant. From the outside looking in, one would think this was a close family relationship. Ethyl and Ralph visit Rick and their daughter-in-law several times a month, but they always call first, and they often bring a small gift. Sometimes they treat the couple to dinner and a movie, saying that it's their pleasure to pay, since they can afford it and Teri and Rick are on such a tight budget.

Recently, however, Teri began to dread her in-laws' visits. Ethyl is barely in the house a minute before she is rearranging furniture or cabinets or even cleaning something. She stacks up the magazines, refolds towels, and even carries out trash. Now that Teri has had a chance to look back on her relationship with Ethyl, she realizes that the "helping hand" was always a rather heavy hand. Ethyl had all but taken over the wedding plans, constantly suggesting that she knew a better way to do this or that. Now Ethyl was certain that she knew the best place for the furniture.

The final blow was wielded the day Ethyl began shining Rick's shoes. When Teri protested, Ethyl insisted that she'd always shined Rick's shoes when he lived at home, and besides, he works *so* hard he shouldn't have to do such menial tasks. (Daughters-in-law always love it when their own jobs and schedules are never acknowledged and what's menial for the husband is viewed as a routine "duty" for her!) Meanwhile, Rick watched as his mother worked up a sweat achieving her spit shine.

By the time they came to me for counseling, this couple were a bundle of tension and anger. Teri went on and on about Ethyl's nosiness. Her mother-in-law wanted to know all Teri and Rick's plans, what they did every day, what they had for dinner, and asked for a rundown of their social life. Even a complete itinerary for their vacations was demanded in advance. Rick doesn't see anything wrong with sharing everything with his parents (even, apparently, his shoes) and has on several occasions discussed issues with them that Teri specifically asked him not to disclose.

Rick came to counseling believing that Teri was out of line. After all, his mother is *kind,* his mother is *generous,* his mother wants only to *help.* He is very sincere in his beliefs. Teri can't understand how Rick can be so blind. Clearly, his mother is undermining her. Ethyl doesn't think Teri is capable of folding towels or stacking magazines and also believes that Rick shouldn't be expected to do these "menial chores." (At least nowadays, most women will fight this attitude, rather than accept it.)

Teri went to stay with a woman friend and agreed to go to counseling only after Rick told her that he wanted to make the marriage work—no matter what. But they didn't reconcile until they'd been in counseling for three months. Teri wouldn't take the chance of having the same patterns start all over again.

It seems odd, but Rick never completely understood Teri's anger at Ethyl. However, he agreed that if it bothered Teri so much, then he should join her in taking a stand. Once she knew that she had her husband's support, Teri could look at Ethyl with a mixture of sadness and humor. She's been able to laugh at Ethyl's old-fashioned beliefs now that she is reassured that Rick doesn't see himself as "king" of the house.

For a little while, Ethyl went along with the new rules her son laid down. But, before long, she began dragging out that cursed shoe polish again. But this time, Teri laughed it off, and now, when her in-laws are due, Rick and Teri line up the shoes and set out the polish. This story has a happy ending, but it's sad that it took a separation before Rick agreed to listen to Teri's concerns.

The above stories happen to deal with mother-in-law/daughter-in-law situations. But similar tensions often occur with fathers-in-law and siblings-in-law, too. And it isn't only the in-law relationships that can become strained. Sometimes, parents can cause trouble by not letting go of their own children.

I once knew a man whose father guided his career, picked out—and paid for—his son's new house, and didn't "allow" his son and daughter-in-law to make their own vacation plans. The daughter-in-law had her own life and didn't care much about tramping around looking at houses anyway, so this wasn't a problem. The vacation destinations were always quite wonderful and her husband seemed fairly happy in his career, so she didn't care about those issues one way or another. This couple ended up in counseling because the husband needed her help in breaking away from his father. She was amazed that he was harboring all these hostile feelings toward his dad. We can live with another person and not even be aware of his or her deepest feelings. With his wife's help, this young man confronted his father, changed careers, and sold the house.

Hurt and angry for a while, the father didn't understand why his son hadn't spoken up before. If he hadn't liked the plans, why didn't he say so? It's a good question, but let's face it, it takes some of us years to learn to stand up for ourselves.

Cards on Monday, Shopping on Wednesday, Dinner on Friday

Jody wishes her husband would spend more time with his buddies. If he did, maybe he wouldn't resent the time she spends with her mother and sisters. They've always played cards on Monday night, they meet in the mall on Wednesday, and they go downtown for dinner on Friday. Jody's father doesn't mind, so why should Steve?

Jenna is sick and tired of keeping their dinner warm while Burt helps his parents with their bills and household chores. Burt says they're too old to do everything by themselves. Besides, he enjoys their company. But Jenna resents having to do all the chores in their house by herself. Burt had a lot of nerve for chiding her about hiring a cleaning service every few weeks. He's too busy with his parents to do his share at home, so how dare he criticize her when she pays someone else to do half the work.

Both couples are heading for trouble, and in fact, Steve did divorce Jody. Two months of counseling proved to Steve that Jody truly preferred her mother's company, and Jody didn't argue with him. She moved back to her mother's house (I think the mother wanted this all along), and now they are free to shop and play cards any time they want. In the last year, another sister has moved back, too. An unhealthy pattern exists here, but until Jody is ready to see it, she can't be a full marriage partner. In fact, she might be a person who never will be a candidate for marriage because she's so comfortable with her mother and sisters. These women might end up living together all their adult lives. Burt and Jenna are working through their difficulties. Jenna stopped fixing big dinners for Burt when she got home from work and chose instead to take a class at the community college and become involved with local political campaigns. She kept the cleaning service, and Burt makes more effort to take care of his share of the household chores. Sometimes she goes to her in-laws' home with Burt and visits with his parents while he does their chores. This pleases Burt because he missed her company.

In most marriages, at times external family pressures call for some sacrifices. I think Jenna's problem was a growing sense of isolation and, perhaps, a feeling that Burt didn't seem to mind spending so much time away. In truth, Burt enjoyed his parents and wanted to help them out, but he hadn't told Jenna that he missed their time together, too. He was pulled in two directions and didn't communicate his feelings very well. Now, however, Jenna understands him better. This was a second marriage for both partners, and they were willing to work hard to patch things up.

In the early years, communication is critical, especially about certain hot-button issues. Who to spend time with and how much time to spend are questions demanding flexibility and a willingness to talk.

Dividing the Time

Samantha and Todd came home from their honeymoon late on Wednesday night. Early on Thursday morning Samantha called her mother to see what she wanted her to bring for the Sunday afternoon get-together. When she got off the phone, Todd commented that he hadn't remembered anything about a plan for Sunday. Before they left for their respective jobs, they were having their first fight as a married couple.

Samantha assumed she and Todd would spend almost every Sunday with her parents. That's what her sisters and their families did. They all watched sports on television, and when the weather was good, they barbecued in the yard. It was fun! She was horrified when Todd said that he preferred to watch sports at home alone, without a bunch of little kids running around. And besides, he wanted to make plans with other couples on Sunday or, perhaps, stay home alone. He thought they'd take some hiking trips, just as they'd done before they were married. He certainly didn't think they'd be with her parents every Sunday.

Samantha was deeply hurt. She took Todd's stance as a rejection of her family. Sure, he said, he liked them all rather well, but did that mean they had to spend their only assured day off with her family? Besides, he has a family, too, and perhaps they could spare a Sunday for them.

Samantha was afraid of hurting her parents, but eventually she understood Todd's point. Without too much difficulty, they agreed to join the crowd on their first Sunday home but told her parents they had other plans for the next Sunday. As it turned out, her parents were disappointed, but hardly devastated. The fear of hurting her mother and father was not based on facts, but on assumptions. Samantha was prepared to dutifully go to her family's home week after week, because she assumed it was expected of her. She had fun with her family, but that's not the point. Without discussing the plan with Todd, she made another assumption; that he would go along with her expectation.

Todd and Samantha used their argument as an impetus to sit down and talk about their expectations about family time. In short, they avoided some future in-law problems because they shared their feelings with each other. Samantha wanted to spend some Sundays with her family, and that was fine with Todd, but he didn't think Samantha should feel duty bound to go. Of course, Samantha and Todd did cause a bit of stir when they took a hiking trip over Thanksgiving, but as Todd pointed out, no one died over it—in either family.

One might wonder why Samantha and Todd hadn't talked about these family issues before the wedding, especially since they had taken weekend trips on a regular basis. However, late or not, they were lucky, because they were willing to dig in and solve the problem when it first appeared. How much time to spend with relatives is just one of many potential areas of conflicts. But I raise it here because it's such a common dilemma, not to mention a source of intense conflict, hurt feelings, and even worse, divided loyalties.

They're Your Parents, You Take Care of Them

About twice a month, Arny invited his parents to visit for a few days. After he'd issued the invitation, he'd tell his wife, Stacy, when the folks were coming, and she would shop for the food they liked and prepare the meals. She'd clean up the house, too, as well as cancel any plans she had made. Arny thought it would be rude if she left the house when his parents were there. Of course Arny left, but according to him, Stacy was in charge of the house and the work involved in keeping it up, so it didn't matter if he left for his golf game on Saturday afternoon. Stacy was there to keep his parents company, and he was always home on time for dinner, which, of course, Stacy cooked.

At first, Stacy accepted this role as normal and she didn't

challenge it. But as her life became busier, her relationship with her visiting in-laws became more strained, too. It was inconvenient for her to cancel her plans just because they happened to be coming for a visit, one which she had nothing to do with planning. Besides, she had never got along very well with them in the first place. After many years of this, her boldness grew along with her discontent. So one day Stacy said, "Why do you leave the house when your parents are here, and yet you expect me to be home to keep them company?" At first, Arny ignored the question and pretended everything was the same. But before her in-laws came for their next visit, she *demanded* that Arny stay home and keep them company—she had other plans, and she wasn't changing them. He was astounded by her demand, and a big argument started. Years of Stacy's repressed, hostile feelings about Arny's parents and the unequal division of responsibilities in the marriage came spilling out.

This couple managed to work out their problems, but had they not decided to go to counseling, the marriage might have ended. Stacy was that angry, and Arny was that oblivious to her feelings. I've heard similar stories about one person taking responsibility for the other person's family members. For example, Fran, married about eighteen months, told me that her sister-in-law, Ellie, was furious that her children's birthdays weren't acknowledged for an entire year. "Why are you telling me about the problem you're having with Bill?" Fran asked. "Talk to him; he's in charge of taking care of your family's gifts. I have all I can do to take care of my own family's birthday cards and presents."

Well, really. How nervy! Ellie couldn't stop talking about that witchy Fran. Who did she think she was? Ellie took care of buying her husband's family their gifts, and she had expected Fran to take on that role when she married Bill. But Fran would have none of it. Unfortunately, the dear brother in this scenario couldn't seem to get it together to get those adorable nieces and nephews their presents. Fed up, Fran told Ellie that if other people hadn't stepped in and covered for Bill, he might have grown up knowing that buying gifts and cards was an adult responsibility. Naturally, Ellie didn't like their family's "ways" being challenged by this upstart sister-in-law, and war was declared.

Bill didn't understand what the fuss was all about. If Ellie would only remind him, he'd run out to the mall and buy the gifts himself. Fran suggested that he enter the kids' birthdays into the computer and check the calendar now and then. That way, Ellie wouldn't be put in a position to have to remind Bill—year after year. That suited Bill just fine. So, a high-tech solution was found for a low-tech—and ancient—problem.

———

I THINK it's best to work out an equitable arrangement about respective responsibilities for taking care of the other person's family before the battleground becomes soaked with angry tears. It's amazing that these expectations can carry over from one generation to another, and in some families, it's assumed that women are in charge of keeping track of social and family occasions. In some situations, they're even in charge of all the thank-you notes! But this old system often doesn't work well today. Like Fran, many women are willing to keep track of their own nieces and nephews, but when they took their marriage vows, they didn't sign on as a social secretary for two families.

In many families, women still do much of the cooking and shopping, but they may not want to cook special dishes for two families, especially if these demanding visits are frequent. We'll continue to see resentful women and their bewildered husbands show up for marriage counseling if these issues aren't addressed early on.

Problems over holiday plans often go hand in hand with other family issues and responsibilities. And if war can break out over birthday gifts, that's nothing compared with what can happen over holidays. Holiday misunderstandings are common early in a marriage, particularly if the issues haven't been resolved before the wedding day.

Turkey for Lunch, Turkey for Dinner

Ira had promised his mother that he'd always spend Thanksgiving Day with her. This was her favorite family day, and he'd never let her down. Ira was sure Debby, his bride of three months, would want to please him, and the Friday after the holiday would certainly satisfy her parents. Ira was in for a big surprise. After casually announcing "their" plans, Debby began screaming: "How dare you make those plans without consulting me? My family makes a big deal out of Thanksgiving, too. I have no intention of missing it, and that's all there is to it."

This was another "first fight," and they ended it by compromising—sort of—and at first, it sounded like a fair solution. The couple spent part of the day with Debby's parents and part of it with Ira's mother. It worked well the first year, so they continued the arrangement, even when it meant bundling up babies and toddlers and taking them to two houses. But now, as the kids get older, it's more difficult to get them to politely eat two feasts within a few hours. Neither set of grandparents shows much understanding when the kids say they can't eat another bite of turkey. "Just try a little harder," one grandma says. Both Debby and Ira wonder just how much longer they can keep this up.

Death Threats and Drama

Holiday traditions are lovely, and we all have a few we cherish, but when carried too far, they can be a source of conflict and tension. Therapists' offices are filled with people who agonize over how not to hurt someone else's feelings, and just as frequently, these offices are filled with those whose feelings have been hurt over holiday issues. People often become so invested in one plan, one way to do things, that they can't see the obvious. When I was telling the Ira and Debby story to an acquaintance, her ten-year-old daughter said, "Why couldn't Ira's mother just go with them to Debby's house?" Out of the mouths of babes. . . .

Since I know this young couple fairly well, I told them that a child, with no ax to grind, had come up with the perfect solution. "Oh no, we can't do that," Ira said, a nervous tone in his voice. "My mother invites her sister, and she wouldn't want to go to a stranger's house."

"My relatives aren't strangers," Debby said. "I think it's worth a try."

"You don't understand—she would be so hurt."

And so it goes. But I've talked with many people about holiday solutions, and some of the best plans involve combining families, inviting friends outside the family to join the celebration, organizing communal dinners at churches or temples, and leaving town and forgetting the whole thing. (If the latter sounds extreme, don't forget that you have a choice about participating. In fact, a couple I know are heading to Mexico this December just to break the pattern dictating that every family member must be present at the big holiday gathering. Resorts and cruise ships are often booked up during holidays—and *lack* of family isn't the only motivation to get away.)

Over the years I've heard people describe mandatory holiday appearances in highly dramatic terms. Here are some examples—see if any sound familiar:

* "My mother will *kill* me if we don't show up for Easter—she loves Easter."

* "Your father will have another *heart attack* if you go anywhere else for Passover."

* "It's the biggest holiday of the year, and I'll be *sick for a week* if we can't see you."

* "She's counting on us. She'll just *die* if we don't show up."

* "You'll *spoil* your brother's *whole* Memorial Day weekend visit by being so selfish. He can only get here twice a year, you know."

* "I'll never get over it. How can you be so cruel to make other plans? I'm serious—I'll *never forgive* you."

So, people will become ill for days, others will be murdered, still others will probably drop dead, and you will ruin someone's life permanently, all because you committed the unforgivable sin of not showing up for a holiday event. Or perhaps you didn't serve the right food or wear the right clothes—a federal offense for sure. Or you made other plans before you knew your older brother was going to be in town, and now everyone's lives are *ruined*.

Weddings and holidays trigger this kind of hyperbole. When we're newly married, we often take these exaggerated exclamations seriously. A newlywed couple, Lori and Adam, had a difficult time believing me when I expressed doubt that Adam's father would really be sick for a week if the couple didn't drive six hundred miles on Christmas Eve just to see him for a few hours. They'd have to drive back home on Christmas Day, because both had to be at work the next day. Lori thought this was nuts, not to mention dangerous.

I agreed with Lori. "Your father is exaggerating for effect, Adam," I said. "People talk about dying or having their lives ruined all the time. It's holiday talk, and you can't be blackmailed by it." Adam looked uncomfortable. He was sure his father was serious about taking to his bed for a week. Some people truly believe they'll cause a parent's heart attack or ruin someone's life over a holiday.

Excessive jealousies, demands, and especially threats have no place being mixed up with family events that are supposed to be fun. I'm convinced that many people choose ski or golf trips, cruises, and camping trips just to remove themselves from the frenzied and emotionally charged atmosphere that surrounds holidays. The fact is, twelve-hundred mile round trips and eating two—or more—holiday dinners and canceling plans with the other person's family usually involve some kind of blackmail.

───────

THE best time to talk about these issues is before the wedding—I can't emphasize this enough. Every family has different traditions, and nowadays, many marriage partners may celebrate some different holidays. If you're the newly married couple, decide together how you would like to handle these holiday events. Are you willing to compromise? Can you visit one family one year and another the next? Can you invite both families to your house? Could all the relatives go out for the holiday dinner?

If you are the parents and in-laws, understand that you could be putting too much pressure on your child. She or he has another family now, and that family has traditions, too. Flexibility is the best policy. Unconventional holiday celebrations can often be the most fun. If they involve your in-law child's religion, these celebrations can be interesting, and at times, even enriching. Traditions are not static; they change with the generations. We may not always like this, but a loving attitude is called for as we make our adjustments.

What could be as stressful as holiday plans? Try money. Bitterness and heartache result if we aren't clear about financial arrangements between families.

Paying the Piper

Kevin and Andrea thought they'd be able to pay back the loan for a down payment on their house within a few years. Kevin's parents didn't hesitate to loan the money, because things were tight for the young couple, and they were sure they'd get the money back. But then, one of the cars broke down, they had a baby, and Andrea needed to leave her job to stay home with the baby. No money was left over, so paying back the loan would just have to wait.

As the years passed, Kevin's parents began thinking about retirement and relocation. Soon they would need the money. "Next year," Kevin said, "next year we'll be in better shape." And so the parents waited another year. Meanwhile, Kevin was troubled that he had to put his parents off. But Andrea thought her in-laws were being selfish. Certainly they knew how tight things were for them. They didn't expect her to go back to work just to pay that silly little loan, did they? Would they hurt their grandchild that way?

So, you see, things can become complicated. From what I can tell, many loans made to children aren't paid back. If money is tight, the credit card bill, the mortgage, or the dental bills are paid first. My advice is generally to avoid lending money to one's children. Either give them the money as a gift or arrange a legal note, with a regular payback schedule. That way it becomes business, not a personal transaction. However, parents should not risk financial insecurity to loan or give money to their adult children. In extreme situations, some help might be necessary, but short of true hardship, I don't recommend it.

When wealthier parents offer gifts to their children, they should do so in a generous spirit and *with no strings attached.* Sometimes a parent's idea of generosity might not be the same as a grown child's.

This Table Has Too Many Strings

Lola and Gene began saving money for a dining room table they really loved. They didn't have to wait long. Gene's parents, Maxine and Ray, said they'd be delighted to buy the table as a gift. As Maxine said, "I'd rather have you enjoy my money now, not when I'm dead. This way, I can have the pleasure of seeing you happy."

Lola had always easily accepted Maxine's gifts before. But the table turned out to be a different story. Maxine decided that now that Gene and Lola's home was complete, the couple could begin entertaining relatives and family friends. The house was filled with beautiful things, many purchased by Maxine herself. Maxine hadn't thought about the fact that Lola was rather shy, and her idea of entertaining was having a few friends in for coffee and dessert or a potluck.

So, without consulting Lola, Maxine began planning the big event. Lola was overwhelmed with the elaborate plans, and she asked Gene to help explain to Maxine that she didn't want to have this party. But Gene only said, "Hey, we owe it to her. She bought the table and so much stuff in our house. Now she wants to show it off. Let her have her fun."

Lola went along with Gene's wishes and had the party. But this wasn't the end of the story. As time went on, Lola noticed that Gene felt obligated to go along with his parents on many occasions, from holidays to weekend invitations to vacations they didn't want to take. So, they trekked around, from Maine to Mexico, being "shown off" to Maxine's friends. Each time Gene said, "We owe it to her."

Lola may be shy, but she's not weak. Eventually, she told Gene that she didn't want more gifts, if each one had a new string attached to it. Gene is afraid of hurting his mother's feelings, and their arguments are getting more intense. Right now I don't know what's going to happen to this couple. Lola refused to go on the last cruise, preferring to save her vacation time for a trip she *wants* to take. Gene went without her and came home angry.

Until this couple sets limits on gifts and Gene clarifies the issues of the "strings," this couple will continue fighting. At the moment, the ties that bind this couple are looking quite loose.

Trouble Spots Can Appear Anywhere

I can't possibly cover all the areas where conflict can rear its head. The stories you've read here represent a few key sensitive spots, however. It's important to understand that not all problems are caused by in-laws, children, and parents, although we often like to find a scapegoat. The problems often indicate areas of misunderstanding and discontent in the marriage itself. Most people experience jealousies and resentments from time to time, and better communication can usually get couples through the rough patches. I don't recommend letting problems build, however. Talk about issues when they first come up.

Some people in the world are simply negative, and after you have made reasonable attempts to work the problems out, it's sometimes better to avoid people who do nothing but poison relationships. You can also seek counseling to help you discuss the issues with an objective person. At times in my own life an objective person could have helped me solve in-law problems.

If you are trying to *prevent* in-law problems or you are trying to solve some that have already started, keep in mind the guidelines below.

For the couple:

1. **Set limits and make rules together—you're a team now.** The two of you may have different ideas, values, and traditions, but you married each other because you wanted to spend your lives together, and therefore, you must learn to respect your differences.

2. **Be willing to compromise.** You may need to give up some of your traditions now and then, but having it all your own way does not constitute a marriage. Compromise is the only road to long-term happiness.

3. **Jointly agree that the relationship between you and your partner is primary.** Most of the time, you won't need to choose between your partner and your family. You are both entitled to family loyalty, but not at the expense of each other. If your partner tells you his or her feelings

are hurt, then don't brush that off. That's a serious statement and deserves consideration. Too often, we tell people how they should or should not feel. When we make attempts to listen to others, they feel validated.

4. **Avoid criticizing your partner's family.** Think twice before you tell your partner that his brother is a jerk or her mother is stupid. Most of us defend our relatives, even if we know the criticism is accurate. Focus instead on what you want and how you would like to be treated.

5. **Put a stop to your family's criticism of your partner.** Make your own decisions about problems with your partner and don't be pressured by your family's declaration that they know what's right for you. Only you know what's right for you.

6. **Support each other—stand as a team.** If partners agree on boundaries, limits, and rules and stand firmly together, other family members will have little choice but to accept. (They won't die, kill you, get sick, or otherwise be harmed.)

7. **Take responsibility for your own family.** Your partner may not feel as strongly as you do about your family. That's okay. When mutual love develops between families and their in-laws, consider it icing on the cake. Feel free to spend some independent time with your family and don't hold it against your partner if he or she prefers not to go along to *every* event and gathering. Don't expect your partner to cater to your family without support from you, and take responsibility for keeping track of your own relatives' graduations and birthdays.

8. **Don't borrow money unless you intend to pay it back.** This does not mean that you *think* you'll pay it back. Borrow the money as if you were borrowing from a

bank. Consider it to be an obligation as important as your mortgage or rent.

9. **Don't accept gifts from family unless they come without strings attached.** Back each other up on this. When a gift has strings, it's called a bribe.

10. **Don't make unnecessary demands on your parents.** Your parents aren't a bank, nor is their house a restaurant or a place you can take charge of, mess up, and then leave. As an adult, you are responsible for yourself, and besides, your parents have lives of their own.

11. **Be prepared to make decisions that won't please parents and/or in-laws.** You can't set limits or make decisions about your life without ever hurting someone's feelings. Your parents may even be angry, but you're an adult now, too. Be gentle but firm as you state your limits.

12. **Talk about problems as they come up.** Don't let small hurts become huge problems. Screaming matches inevitably result when problems fester. Try to determine if problems are truly about your parents or in-laws or whether they reflect problems in your relationship.

13. **Be prepared to distance yourselves if necessary.** You've tried everything, and nothing works. The negativity is causing so many problems that you must pull away to preserve your relationship. Explain your reasons and spend less time with the troublesome relative. It isn't pleasant, but no one benefits from negativity that can't be changed.

14. **Include your parents and in-laws in your life whenever possible.** Parents want their children to be part of their lives. It's a natural desire. Marriage means greater independence, but it doesn't mean the end of the parental bond. A parent or in-law relationship can be rich and

deeply rewarding. Remember, you might find yourself in your parents' shoes one day.

For the parents:

1. **Make rules together.** You and your spouse should discuss the relationship with the new in-law. Make sure you agree about respecting his or her traditions, values, ideas, and background.

2. **Be willing to compromise.** Your children will inevitably resent you if you make unreasonable demands and show disrespect for the in-law child's traditions and values. Compromise is the key to harmonious relationships.

3. **Don't take sides.** If the partners are having a disagreement, don't jump in on one side or the other. When they solve their problem, you might look like the problem, and forgiveness may not come easily, if at all.

4. **Don't be critical of your child's partner.** This is a corollary to the above suggestion. You may think you know what's best for your adult child, but that's probably not true. You could be wrong about your in-law child, and even if your child does make a mistake, it's his or her mistake to make.

5. **Don't lend adult children money.** Ideally, give a no-strings-attached gift of money if it's needed. Less ideally, draw up a legal contract and have payments go to a bank account. Money issues involving relatives often lead to resentments and misunderstandings. Your family isn't immune to a nearly universal experience.

6. **Give your kids space.** Wait for an invitation before you visit, or at least ask if you can see them. Make sure that the time is good for both partners, unless you have a specific plan to visit with just one.

7. **Offer no advice unless it's asked for.** When asked, state your opinion—once. If your advice is ignored, forget about it.

8. **Don't make assumptions about what you're allowed to do in their home.** They should treat your home with respect, and you should give them the same courtesy. Always ask permission before you rummage through the kitchen cabinets looking for a plate or you change the channel on the television.

9. **Don't make unnecessary demands about holidays and traditions.** Two families have joined together now, and you might not like the other family's traditions. Even if you aren't pleased with the arrangements, try to be understanding. The compromises the new couple make aren't really any of your business anyway. This isn't always easy to accept, but to take a different stance is to risk alienation.

10. **No guilt trips allowed.** The worst thing you can do is convince grown children to do something out of guilt. Sure, you got your way this time, but the long-term price is high.

11. **Talk about issues when they come up.** Brooding in silence is no fun for anyone. Furthermore, problems don't just go away. If you and your child or in-law child are having trouble, try talking about it. See if you can smooth the problems out early in the relationship.

You might conclude that these rules apply across the board, not just during the early years of marriage. You're right. However, if you follow them from the beginning, you'll have fewer difficulties down the road. When we insult or hurt a parent or in-law, even unwittingly, it can take years to repair the damage. If we keep these suggestions in mind, however, we can look forward to more harmony and take pleasure in the new family the wedding created.

One day, you may find you are a new parent or a new grandparent. In the next chapter, we'll discuss the ways grandchildren create yet another shift in the in-law relationship.

5 THE GRANDEST TIE:
When In-Laws Become Grandparents

*M*y husband and I have always enjoyed a wide circle of friends and an active social life. But, some years ago, we began to stoically resign ourselves to the time during an evening when handbags were searched, wallets opened, and pictures of the grandchildren emerged. The conversation inevitably shifted to descriptions of how extraordinary, accomplished, and beautiful these little human wonders were. Naturally, with great enthusiasm we admired the photos, and we quickly agreed that these truly were exceptional children.

Later, when we were alone, Fred and I admitted being amused by these zealous grandparents, who before these miraculous births were just regular folks like the rest of us. Now that their children had produced "wonder babies," they were transformed into bizarre beings who marveled over a baby's first smile and who bragged when these precocious infants learned to roll over, not to mention the obvious genius revealed in the baby's first "patty cake." (The most photographed babies in the world must be the first grandchild in every family.)

Fred and I laughed when our friends told us that their granddaughter was the smartest child in the kindergarten or the best dancer in ballet class. And could so many one-day-to-be-legendary pitching arms and slam dunkers be developing on second grade sports teams all over the country?

Well, about ten years ago, something exciting happened to Fred and me. Our daughter had a baby. You just had to see this baby to believe her. Brittany was the most alert and active newborn in the hospital nursery—and by far the most beautiful! Later, when she rolled over, it was a wonder to behold, and her smile was the most radiant of any baby ever born—even our own daughter's. Soon after Brittany was born, we became grandparents again and yet again. So, as chance would have it, we have three of the best-looking and certainly the brightest grandchildren ever born. And, just in case visual proof is needed, we have several pictures of each of them with us at all times. Of course, our friends are thrilled to look at the latest pictures over dinner in a restaurant. No one can resist these adorable faces.

So much for our resolve not to become "typical" grandparents. If you are a grandparent, you will understand this radical change in our behavior. In general, the change is about reexperiencing a certain type of love. We can love many people during the course of our lives, and the more individuals we love, the happier we generally are. But the love for a child is particularly special, perhaps the most special love of all. A parent's intense and unconditional love for a child is expected, but the wonder of its profound nature never ceases to amaze me. Consider the image of parents whose children are accused of even the most heinous crimes. They will always say that they love their children no matter what!

Perhaps the only love that is expressed even more intensely than the love parents have for their children is the deep feelings these parents have for their grandchildren. It is true that something happens when parents become grandparents—they go crazy! If you have any doubt about this, read on. I've seen grandparents do things with and for their grandchildren they never would have considered doing for their children. And these things seem quite normal, so normal that grandparents might be extremely offended at the suggestion that their doting is excessive.

You're Moving Where?

When the last of their three children left for college, Eric and Marcia sold their big house with the perfect yard for growing children and moved into a small, economical town home. No more lawn to mow or gutters to clean! To close friends, they even admitted that they were pleased to have an empty nest, and they happily left their kids alone to build their own nests. But then their son and daughter-in-law had one of these special creatures called a baby.

Within six months, Eric and Marcia had sold the town house (no yard to play in, you know) and bought a three-bedroom house only two blocks from their son's home (makes it easier on the kids when they need a baby-sitter for Alex or when they visit, which will undoubtedly be weekly, if not daily). What were they thinking, they said to themselves, when they sold their house? And their kids must have felt so rejected a couple of years ago when they went on a golfing vacation over the Thanksgiving holiday instead of having the whole family over for dinner. Well, all that's changed now. Holidays are for families, and each one must be special for little Alex.

If this sounds extreme or unusual, I assure you that I have seen many otherwise rational adults change their lifestyle when they become grandparents. With their first peek at the new baby, they often form an immediate and powerful bond. Even if these parents have not seen much of their grown children in recent years, they rethink that relationship now. They may—quite suddenly—want to spend more time with their children because that means increased access to their precious grandchildren. (The real reason behind some of this newfound interest is usually not lost on the grown kids.)

Many grandparents have reached a time in their lives when the demands of career and family have lessened, and they may have more free time than ever before. Obviously, this isn't always the case, particularly among younger grandparents whose retirement years are far in the future. But many grandparents are retired, and because of reduced responsibilities, they may have plenty of money as well as time. Many are only too eager to spend both on their grandchildren. After all, who is in a better position to indulge and pamper these children than they are?

The Many Faces of "Doting"

Indulgent and doting grandparents are very common, but the reasons for heaping attention, and often material things too, on grandchildren are varied. For example, overindulgence may be a way—often unconscious—of making amends for what went wrong when raising one's children. I know many grandparents who want to give lavishly because they are still carrying guilt about not doing everything perfectly with their own children. But now that they are grandparents, they finally have a chance to "get it right." Sometimes the birth of a child is a distraction for a grandparent, who may be facing retirement or whose career is winding down.

Regardless of the reason, the dose of enthusiasm sparked by becoming a grandparent is usually welcomed by the new parents, who are often overwhelmed and struggling to adjust. (They usually want to do everything perfectly, too.) At first, new mothers may find the presence of their own mothers comforting and reassuring. Sons may find a new closeness with their fathers. Sometimes, however, the ties that bind parents and children may begin to feel a bit too tight as grandparents become more involved in the lives of their grandchildren. Resentments may surface, and the new parents may show resistance to any attempts to interfere with how they wish to raise their children. They particularly resist the "helpful" advice offered by the in-law grandparents. It is no wonder that this joyous time can become confusing and stressful.

Do They Really Need That?

Six-month-old Janie has enough clothes to outfit twenty babies, which is not surprising since Grandma Becky brings new clothes every time she visits. No matter that Janie doesn't need forty-dollar outfits that she outgrows within weeks anyway. (Where is a baby going to wear these fancy duds?) But now that she finally has some extra money, Becky likes to pick out nice clothes for the baby. She could not afford to do that for her own children. Becky says she is doing this for Janie, but she is insightful enough to realize that she is making up years of deprivation when she was raising her three kids alone. "No matter," she says to her daughter, Jean, "you'll have all these clothes for your next child." Jean, however, is beginning to worry about when this excessive spending is going to end. (She also resents the assumption that there will be a "next child.")

Marge and Jeff also love to shop. They spend hours in the stores, checking out toys and games for their three grandchildren. Jeff especially enjoys those toys that take hours to assemble. Jeff and Marge are retired, and instead of creating a new life for themselves, they fill empty hours with this often-pointless shopping. Indulging their grandchildren seems harmless enough.

Like Becky, Marge and Jeff are not receiving effusive thanks for all their efforts but are, instead, being criticized. At one point, Jean told Becky to "get a life" and quit bringing a shopping bag into the house every time she visits. "Spend the extra money on yourself or ask me what Janie needs before you buy all this stuff." Marge and Jeff's children are disturbed because the children are old enough to look forward to their grandparents' visits, and now they *expect* gifts. In addition, the parents have concerns about paying dental bills and making the mortgage payment. To this struggling couple, it is nonsensical to see their children receive so many expensive video games and the latest "fad" toys when the family is barely able to meet basic expenses.

Many parents, whom we should all remember were raised by the grandparents and whose values were shaped by these now overly indulgent adults, are concerned about the values that are forming when great importance is attached to a grandchild's every whim. Grown children have been known to say things like, "You weren't this way with me. You told me to save my own money for special clothes or a game. Why are you intent on ruining my children's values?" Of course, the grandparents often take issue with this extreme position. As one grandfather said, "I thought it was their job to do the work and my job to have all the fun with the kids. A little indulgence never ruined anyone's values." Well, yes and no. It is all relative, and in general, these decisions should not be left to chance.

One need only look at the advice columns in the newspaper to see how often the generosity of grandparents is bothersome to parents. I recall one letter that described a situation in which the grandchildren received so many gifts from one set of grandparents that the other set stopped bringing any birthday or holidays gifts. They couldn't compete with the expensive and elaborate presents, so they withdrew. Better to bring nothing than to have a gift that was a single tree in a vast forest. So huge was the pile of gifts that the children often forgot some of them by the end of the day. The parents were left with a dilemma about how to stop one set of grandparents from not only spoiling the kids but alienating the other grandparents, too. This is an extreme situation, but I have worked with families who are grappling with variations on this very theme.

Keeping in mind how much joy some grandparents find in shopping for their grandchildren, parents have the right— indeed, the duty—to make some rules. When relationships are generally amiable, perhaps the better word is "guidelines." The most important thing is for the parents of the new baby to decide together what they want and then gently explain the guidelines to the new, and as we've said, slightly ga-ga, grandparents. (Some of these normally balanced adults really do get a bit crazy, so try to understand and not overreact.) Unfortunately, gentle persuasion does not always work.

These Grandmas Are Feuding

Lil and Jeannette are proud, new grandmothers. Lil's daughter gave birth to baby Ryan, but instead of just enjoying the experience, Ryan's entry into their lives has set off a contest over who can capture her love and attention. If Lil visits the baby one day, then Jeannette is sure to come the next. Meanwhile, Simone and Ralph, the new parents, wonder what to do to curb all these visits. Simone liked having both women visit when the baby was born and she was on maternity leave, but now one or the other often shows up unannounced just as she is coming home from work. Ralph works the night shift, and he needs to sleep after taking care of Ryan all day. To say the least, it is most annoying to have Lil asking about Jeannette's last visit and probing about what gift she brought the baby. If Jeannette brings a rattle, then the next day Lil will show up with a teething ring. Neither of these grandmothers is wealthy, which makes this competition even more destructive.

An additional problem comes with these gift-giving grannies. Simone and Ralph are becoming alienated from their mothers because the unplanned visits and the excessive intrusion into their lives is wearing thin. Almost every day, just when they are trying to spend a few minutes together and fuss over the baby as a couple, they have a mother or mother-in-law to contend with. They have asked Lil and Jeannette to call before they visit, but in their selfish efforts to equalize their time with the baby, both grandmothers continue to show up unannounced—gift in hand. Apparently, the grandmothers each come bearing gifts as a way to justify the spontaneous visits. Simone and Ralph end up appearing ungrateful, which makes them even more annoyed. Given that this problem has been going on for many months, it is likely to be resolved only by bringing both grandmothers together and asking (first) and then demanding (if necessary) that they end their rivalry, which is obviously causing this crazy behavior.

Many couples face a variation of the problem that Lil and Jeannette have created. Simone and Ralph are fortunate in that they agree a problem exists, and as a team, they want to solve it. In other words, neither Simone nor Ralph tries to justify the behavior. I have seen too many situations in which one or the other new parent either isn't around for the pop-in visits or doesn't see what the big deal is.

As with all the other issues of marriage, the couple must discuss the desires and demands of both sets of grandparents.

First-time parents, in particular, should anticipate the changes in their relationship after the baby is born but also recognize that relationships with in-laws and parents will inevitably change, too. Having a baby is exciting and may be the fulfillment of a lifelong dream. However, it is a stressful time, and grandparents must understand that their children may be anxious and exhausted. The new parents need support, not demanding and jealous grandparents.

Jealousy Is Not So Unusual

In speaking with grandparents and working with people in all stages of life in my professional practice, I have sometimes been struck by the extent of the jealousy that exists. One common complaint is that sons become closer to the in-law grandparents and abandon their own parents. Remember the saying, "A daughter is a daughter for all her life, but a son is a son 'til he takes a wife."

April, a friend of mine, commented that the birth of her son's first child brought a definite shift in her relationship with her son and daughter-in-law, Kara. She had always been close to Kara, but when Benjamin was born, Kara preferred to have her own mother around when they brought the baby home. Nowadays, with hospital stays so short, the new mother may be very tired and even weak. This was the case with Kara. As vulnerable as she was feeling, it wasn't surprising to April that Kara was eager to have her mother help out. Rusty, the new dad, was pleased, too, because it made Kara happy, and he liked his mother-in-law, Esther. April felt a bit left out, but she was mature enough to realize that, in most cases, a new mother will feel most comfortable having her own mother's help.

As the weeks went by, Kara began asking April to visit more frequently, so she, too, had a chance to bond with and enjoy the baby. April was smart enough to contain her own need to feel useful and important, and she refrained from interpreting Kara's relationship with her own mother as a slight to her.

Velma told me about going to the hospital when she heard that Carly, her daughter-in-law, was in labor. Velma was surprised when she saw not only Carly's mother, but all five of Carly's sisters in the waiting room! The sisters' husbands and boyfriends had been sent out for coffee and sandwiches and had left the women to catch up on all the family news while they waited. While all the women were gracious and welcomed her, Velma realized that the birth of her son Jason's child would mean at least a temporary shift in her relationship with Carly. Truthfully, she was saddened, perhaps because she didn't have a daughter or even a sister. As fond as she was of Carly, she realized that she would never be the "preferred" grandmother at critical times. She kept her thoughts to herself and adjusted, which was very wise, because within two years Carly and Jason were divorced. She sees her grandson regularly, and Carly has always welcomed Velma to family parties and events even though Carly has since remarried. Velma knows that she has a warm relationship with her former daughter-in-law in large part because she made no attempt to compete with Carly's mother and sisters.

In some situations a daughter begins to prefer her in-law family, perhaps because her family is farther away and her husband's family is close by. Sometimes the reason can be as simple as the fact that her mother is still involved with her career and her nonworking mother-in-law is available to help out or baby-sit during the day. Of course, this preference could also develop because a daughter has never been close to her own family and prefers her new relatives. Regardless of the reasons, likely a time of redefining relationships will arrive.

April and Velma were wise to face their feelings rather than deny them. Too often, jealousy, envy, self-pity, a need to feel important, or even a desire to make up for mistakes or circumstances of the past may surface when a grandchild is born. But instead of dealing with the feelings and examining the reasons why these issues have surfaced, adults may justify their behavior and even blame others if something goes wrong. A better way exists. A mother-in-law may see her daughter-in-law's relationship with her mother and have normal feelings of sadness that she never had a daughter of her own. Perhaps she will grieve for a short time, but this doesn't mean that she loves her sons any less. She is simply grieving a missed experience. Or a new grandfather may realize that he neglected his family when he was focused on his career. Now he wants to make it up to his children by doting on their kids. If he is aware that this is happening, he can examine his feelings and resolve to put the needs of the grandchildren—and his children—ahead of his need to feel important. The fact is that recapturing lost time isn't possible. If warring in-laws have a need to outdo each other, who are the losers? The parents and grandchildren, who suffer under the strain.

Who's the Baby?

Parents are fond of telling their children to stop acting like children and "grow up." Well, jealous grandparents can be among the most immature individuals around. When parents begin to feel slighted, they may then vie for the attention and affection of their children and grandchildren in various ways. For example, they may start criticizing their child's in-laws and attempt to manipulate their child to criticize these individuals too.

Other jealous and threatened grandparents may complain that they are neglected or are not loved and appreciated enough (whatever "enough" is), which sounds like the proverbial guilt trip—and it is. Or some grandparents play the martyr role, waiting to be begged to come for a visit. And, as I've described, some childish grandparents are generous to a fault, sometimes even as a way to compete with the other set of grandparents.

Get a Life!

When I work with grandparents who are overinvolved, one way or another, with their grandchildren, I attempt to find the reason for the imbalance in their lives. Why are they sacrificing their money and time for these children, no matter how precious they are? What dreams did they have for their later years? Is this the retirement they envisioned?

Denise came to see me after a troubling realization. Two weeks before our first counseling session, she had withdrawn three hundred dollars from one of her accounts and she was on her way to buy her granddaughter, Carrie, some school clothes. It was not the first time she had done this. It shamed her to think that Abby, her daughter, was going to a clothing exchange for new outfits for Carrie. But Abby was quite happy that the parents in the school held an annual clothing exchange, an event at which the parents of the older children brought outgrown clothes that the younger children could have. How practical! But to Denise, secondhand clothing brought back memories of her own childhood of hand-me-downs. Her children never wore them, and she never expected that Carrie or her other grandchildren would *ever* wear other children's "old" clothes.

Denise was on her way to the children's section of the department store, but before she began choosing the clothes, it occurred to her that she really wasn't thinking about Carrie. Instead, her thoughts were immersed in her own childhood. Denise had the sense to stop long enough to think about the three hundred dollars in her handbag. Was she going to "one up" Abby by buying these clothes? Would Carrie now think that the "new" things from the clothing exchange were second best? Abby had said that the exchange was like a carnival, with games and activities to occupy the kids while the parents went through boxes of clothes. It was supposed to be festive and fun, and the idea was to meet other parents, save some money, and let the kids enjoy wearing each other's clothes. And besides, Denise thought, she didn't have a large retirement fund—and she wanted to retire in about eight years. What was she thinking?

When Denise came to see me, she was worried about her future and the fact that she had done little to plan for a life of her own. While shedding many tears, Denise told me that she now regretted doing so much for Carrie, not because it harmed her, but because she had, in many small ways, undermined Abby's values, as well as those of her son-in-law. Abby and Leif had a good family income, but they saved quite a bit of money and didn't live lavishly—on purpose. And there was Denise, always bringing in more "stuff." On top of all that, she had the realization that her own life was relatively empty.

Denise's story is unfortunately not unusual. Widowed at a fairly young age, she had put energy into raising her two children and in holding down a job she hoped was secure. Now, in her late fifties, she was still ignoring her own needs. What's more, her children weren't thanking her.

FOR some grandparents, the "crazy" stage, where life seems to be consumed with thinking about and chattering about grandchildren, is fairly short-lived. Soon the grandparents are back to their regular activities, taking their own vacations, and so forth. Occasionally, however, the grandparents' lives are out of balance even before the grandchildren arrive. This was the situation with Denise. Her problems went far deeper than simply overindulging a grandchild. Not only was Denise still stuck in resentments about her own childhood, she had forgotten about having dreams and goals herself. Within a few months of working with me, she began to emerge from her shell, and she signed up for a painting class at an adult education center near her office. She bought a treadmill and began a walking program, and she planned a real vacation. "These last years," she said, "I took my vacation when it was convenient for my children. I took care of their children while they got away to relax!"

Marge and Jeff were much like Denise. One doesn't have to be a single grandparent to lack a balanced life. Their preoccupation with shopping was covering up their empty lives. When I work with these grandparents, I remind them that now is the time to do all the things they denied themselves when they were being responsible parents—and usually working hard too. I encourage these men and women, single or married, to make new friends among people in the same stage of life. I also point out that the quality of time they spend with grandchildren is more important than the quantity of time.

Problems are sure to arise when grandparents are overattentive to grandchildren. Aside from ignoring their own lives, they may also begin to assume that they know what's best for the children, even if it means going against the parents.

You Did What?

Like many grandparents, Marvin wants his grandson to have all the advantages he didn't have as a child and was unable to give his own children. Marvin is now in a position to be generous with time and money. Six-year-old Greg has been on fishing and camping trips, to baseball games, and to amusement parks. Every time a new children's movie hits the theaters, Marvin and Greg are first in line. But one day this harmless fun took a turn when Marvin took Greg to the racetrack. He managed to convince his friend, the gatekeeper at the track, to let him in with a child, even though it is illegal to do so. Now Marvin is in danger of losing the privilege of taking Greg anywhere alone. What's next? A casino in Atlantic City?

To Grandpa's Church We Go

Alma and Richard were not pleased when their son married outside the family's faith. They were even less pleased when he converted to his wife's religion. But after many heated arguments, Alma and Richard made the sensible decision to make the best of a situation they could not change. For several years, the in-law relationships were quite pleasant.

The birth of the first grandchild broke the peace. For a year, Richard brooded about the fact that his granddaughter wasn't baptized and would never go to church. Finally, when Marcy was about a year old, he began to take her to his church. He didn't tell anyone, but eventually Marcy learned to talk, and she told her mother about the strange place Grandpa had taken her. Needless to say, Marcy's parents were very angry that their right to choose their child's religion was usurped. It was a long time before these fences were mended.

Do We Need Rules?

In many cases, the boundaries between children and parents over the grandchildren are informal and no firm rules are needed. All the adults involved are sensible, and the grandparents know that these little ones do not belong to them. Occasionally, however, grandparents make serious mistakes, and then rules are unavoidable. It goes without saying that parents have control over the religious education of their children. In today's more tolerant world, many children are exposed to more than one religion, and therefore, fewer problems arise when grandparents want to include the grandchildren in religious events. However, this isn't always the case, and the grandparents must step back and allow the parents their rights.

What about Spoilers Rights?

Some grandparents believe they have spoilers rights. The argument goes like this: Grandparents should be allowed to bend the rules, because it is impossible to be spoiled or influenced by grandparents. Kids just intuitively know that grandparents' rules are more flexible than other rules. Therefore, they will not expect the same special treatment from other adults, especially not their own parents.

I have a confession to make. Not only do I hear this argument frequently, I use it myself as an explanation about why I spoil my grandchildren! I plead, along with other grandparents, to let the parents be the tough ones and allow me to spoil and indulge the children. I'm sure that part of the rationale is that spoiling the kids provides an opportunity to perhaps make up for our own deficiencies as parents. Or maybe we do it because it pleases us, and we like to see the grandkids happy.

That said, I must also add that I do understand parents' concerns. Grandparents must be careful not to send the wrong message. Children are impressionable, and grandparents can be powerful role models. What message do we send if we appear to be "sneaking" something behind the parents' backs? Beyond that, children who have every request fulfilled, no matter by whom, may never learn that they can't have everything they want. These children are difficult at home and at school. I would not want to see any child indulged and spoiled in this way, including my own much-loved grandchildren. Therefore, the bottom line remains. The parents should have the final say in setting limits and making rules. Of course, we hope that these children we raised are understanding and will not deny us the pleasure of at least some giving. The moral of the story is: Let's compromise. Given the rapid pace of change in our society, compromise is called for in many areas.

What an Odd Situation—Or Is It?

Franny and Cliff have Josie, a lovely baby girl. She is a very lucky little girl because she has lots of grandparents. Of course, some of the grandparents don't approve of each other—or of Franny and Cliff. So who are all these people? First we have Franny's mother and father and her stepmother and stepfather. Then we have Cliff's mother and her brand new husband, plus her second husband, who has been like a father to Cliff, and then we have the second husband's new live-in friend. Cliff's biological father is around, too, although not as much as Cliff's stepfather. Oh, and let's not forget that Cliff has a great-grandmother who is alive and well and in her seventies. She loves doting on the baby, too!

Franny's brood has always thought Cliff's bunch is sort of odd. Most of this group are just as happy that Franny and Cliff haven't married. For the most part, Cliff's family members are afraid that Franny will run off with Josie if they don't marry.

If this situation sounds a bit chaotic and even odd, remember that blended families are very common today. Some grandchildren have more than four grandparents, and of course, some start out with fewer than four. In itself, this is not a problem. After all, if a degree of harmony exists among the configuration of parents and stepparents, then it simply means that more adults are available to love a baby—and that can't hurt.

In addition, it is not unusual to become a grandparent when the parents of the beloved children are not married or may not even live together. In my experience rarely do both partners' parents agree in either their approval or disapproval. Usually someone has something to say, and many people are trying to influence the couple's future plans.

Pat and Frieda are at odds. Both are grandparents much earlier than expected. Pat's daughter, Ivy, who is seventeen, lives with her. Pat helps Ivy take care of her son, Alan, who has just had his first birthday. Alan's father is Steven, who just turned eighteen. His parents are Frieda and Craig. Pat and Ivy invited Frieda and Craig to come to Alan's birthday party with Steven—and any other relatives they wanted to invite. Frieda refused, however, and tried to keep Steven away, too. She wanted to have a separate party for Alan, with only her relatives attending. Pat suggested that Frieda and Craig host Alan's second birthday party. Frieda exploded at that suggestion, and in her angry outburst, even implied that she was planning to help Steven get custody of Alan. Naturally, this sent Ivy into a frenzy of accusations against Steven, who claimed complete innocence of his mother's "secret plan." Oh my. Does this group need family counseling or what?

This story sounds bizarre unless you have presided over

a counseling session with a group of people in this much trouble, in which case you realize that it is just one more type of situation some families face today. The fact is, Ivy and Steven, who have a very hard road ahead of them, need the support and cooperation of both sets of parents. Pat has been very friendly to Steven, and she hopes that Steven and Ivy will eventually marry. Meanwhile, Frieda admitted that she thought Ivy was a tramp—not good enough for Steven anyway. (How *did* that girl get pregnant?) And according to Frieda (with Craig cheering from the sidelines), little Alan should be with his father. Steven has had to convince Ivy that he has no intention of taking the baby away from her. Ivy is a good mother, and Pat is a big help. Both young people need to finish school and plan for their separate futures because, despite Pat's hopes, they are no longer romantically involved. Right now, Steven's parents are risking being cut off from Alan because of their attitude toward Ivy and Pat. Tragically, this situation has not yet resolved itself.

The Way It Used to Be

No doubt some people will hear stories like Ivy and Steven's and think, "What's happened to our culture? It was never like this before." Well, yes and no. As a friend of mine pointed out, it wasn't like this in the past because the stigma against single mothers and fathers was so severe that a young person like Ivy would have felt forced to release her baby for adoption. In some situations, the father of the baby never knew he had a child. As a therapist, I have heard all about the so-called good ol' days. I've seen women—and some men—anguish over their relinquished children, and they live for a chance to meet them later in life. So, while it may not be easy to learn that your unmarried child is going to be a parent, in today's more open society, you have the possibility to enjoy a relationship with the grandchild. Of course, the amount of support and help you offer is a matter of personal choice.

Not every single parent is a teenager. I've known women in their thirties and forties who have children on their own. The grandparents involved have often been shocked, but sometimes pleasantly surprised, too, that they have this unexpected new member of the family. In some cases, the father's family is often just as eager as the mother's family to bond with the baby. The point, of course, is that as parents we do not have any control over how our grandchildren arrive. We may be grandparents earlier than expected and in circumstances that we don't consider ideal. We may have one grandchild when we hoped for more. Some of our grandchildren may be adopted and perhaps from different racial or ethnic backgrounds. Our grandchildren may be step-grandchildren. In the end, it doesn't matter. The same joys are possible, and the same "rules" apply.

The Perfect Sitter

In most cases, grandparents make the best baby-sitters. They can be trusted, they aren't strangers, and they love the children so much that they will give their all to the job whether it's for an hour or a week. Unless physical limitations exist, grandparents usually are the most watchful and concerned caregivers, which is why parents like to leave their children with grandparents. But, even in the best situations, potential problems arise.

A Cry for Help

An angry and sad Alex and Rosie came to me for counseling. Rosie's gynecologist had referred them because Rosie was diagnosed with postpartum depression. Their son, Kyle, was only six weeks old, but Rosie was so exhausted that she couldn't take care of him alone. This was bitterly disappointing to this young couple, who had envisioned being tired but happy and content with the birth of their first child. Neither had anticipated how hard it would be to care for the baby, and they certainly hadn't anticipated Rosie's difficult adjustment.

Rosie did indeed look tired as she explained how exhausted she was. She was also frustrated because she had no time for herself, not to rest and certainly not to read a book or even do her nails. While Kyle was awake, Rosie was busy every minute, and when he was asleep, Rosie was anxious and tense as she waited for him to awaken.

Alex showed his disgust as Rosie talked. He shot verbal barbs at his wife, sending a clear message that her complaints were trivial. How, he wondered, could an infant who sleeps most of the time exhaust anyone? Besides, he claimed, Rosie was the one who had pressured him to have a baby, so surely she should make the sacrifices.

The atmosphere in my office became increasingly hostile as these partners blamed each other for their problems. It took great effort to calm them down, but eventually they managed to talk to each other with relative civility. I told them that many new parents feel as they do and have the same problems. In fact, it is a "dirty little secret" in our society that feeling disappointed and frustrated after a new baby arrives is quite common. And almost all new parents experience some ambivalence, but rarely do they discuss it.

Eventually, Alex admitted that the baby *was* a lot of work, and he also confessed that he had not expected his lifestyle to change so dramatically. And he surprised Rosie by saying that he was jealous of the time and attention she gave to Kyle. For her part, Rosie spoke out about her resentment and anger that the burden of the new baby was entirely on her shoulders. After all, she said, Alex could leave the house any time he felt like it and "escape" to his job without any concern about the baby's care.

Once they had discussed their inner feelings they could think about solutions to their problem. One solution involved Rosie's mother, Helen, who was just waiting for a chance to spend more time with her new grandson. She eagerly agreed to baby-sit so that Rosie could get out more or just have a break at home. This sounds good; but what went wrong?

Throw Out the Book—And Mom, Too

Oh my. It didn't take long for Helen to take over! And why not? She'd had four children, so she knew everything about babies. And if some little fact she didn't know came up, she had the best book on the market, *Keeping Baby Happy Every Minute,* to consult. The first thing she did was change Kyle's feeding schedule. When Rosie suggested that perhaps Kyle was being fed too often, Helen whipped out her book and pointed out the passages that endorsed demand feeding. Then Helen spent several hours a day with Kyle on the patio, because as everyone knows, babies need fresh air. Rosie suggested that Kyle could skip the fresh air on very cold days. Helen said no. Not only is fresh air good for you, each of her children had been outside every day of their infancy, and look how healthy each is.

Helen also believed that an infant should never be awakened from his sleep. This rule created an angry row between mother and daughter, because if Rosie was out for several hours, she wanted to see the baby when she came back. But Helen wouldn't allow it.

Now we had these battles to deal with. Mother and daughter fought constantly over what was right for Kyle. Alex became involved too, and he chose sides based on how he assessed the relative merits of each issue. Before long, Helen, who was once close to Rosie and Alex and considered a loving parent, was now viewed as an opinionated and interfering mother and mother-in-law.

Resolution came only after Rosie and Alex discussed the situation alone and came up with their "policies." They made it clear to Helen that they would hire a sitter if she didn't go along. Helen protested and carried on, but in the end, she wanted to be with Kyle, so she agreed. But she still maintained that she was right—that she knew best.

Does Anyone Really Know Best?

We live in a world of experts. Perhaps the most plentiful experts are those who tell us how to raise children. Unfortunately, the experts often have ideas that are diametrically opposed. These differing opinions then cause parents to wonder which way is right. Grandparents may get involved in the act as well, and then they risk being accused of being that awful word, "interfering."

Parents and in-laws often think they know what is best for their grandchildren. Sometimes they are right—they do know better because no better teacher exists than experience. Sometimes grandparents claim to know how to "do it right" because they made so many mistakes themselves! Now they just want to help their children avoid making those same mistakes.

It can be helpful for grandparents to offer some advice, and the children may ask questions. My advice is to offer suggestions *once* and then leave it alone. If parents decide to do things their own way, which is their prerogative, then they don't need the added burden of what could feel like criticism. The fact is, we do learn from mistakes, and parenting is a role in which much needs to be learned. If children view the grandparents as critical, then they may not be welcome, or the visits will be limited and the atmosphere strained.

The Exception to the Rule

An important exception to the "non-interference rule" needs to be stated. It is our duty as citizens, not just family members, to report child abuse when we are aware of it. If you are a grandparent and you believe your grandchild is being physically, emotionally, or sexually abused, you are obligated to interfere. (Verbal abuse is not covered by law; however, if you believe your grandchild is suffering from verbal abuse, seek the advice of a counselor to determine how you can effectively intervene.) This is the one time when family ties are not the most important issue; obviously, more important are the safety and well-being of your grandchild. And common sense must prevail. I've heard of grandparents claiming abuse when their grandchild was being raised in a religion they did not approve of or in a communal situation or in some other unconventional circumstance. In most cases, unconventional child rearing does not equal abuse. If the child is being well cared for and is physically healthy, then make the best of the situation. True abuse is covered by laws in every state. I recommend seeking the support of a counselor in order to determine if abuse really is occurring before you contact authorities. This book is not about child abuse, so I will stop here. But let your own heart be your guide in this issue.

Mom, I Need a Baby-Sitter!

Alicia was furious with her mother. Now that her new baby, Cindy, was old enough to be left with a sitter once in a while, Alicia assumed her mother, Elena, would be happy to be that sitter. After all, Elena, a widow with free time on her hands, loved her grandchildren. She'd happily taken care of the three children that belonged to Alicia's brother and sister. Naturally Alicia was upset when her mother turned down the request to baby-sit. "I'm not doing that so much anymore," Elena said.

Alicia was hurt about the refusal, but she was also resentful of her mother's new attitude. Lately, Alicia noticed, Elena had become vain and self-indulgent. She had lost some weight and even dyed her hair red. Imagine that! And she had joined a ballroom dance club. Elena admitted that she wasn't baby-sitting because she was spending time with the new man in her life!

It isn't fair, Alicia thought. Elena did so much baby-sitting for the other grandchildren, and now it was her turn to get the help. Elena explained that she had spent a good many years mourning the death of her husband, Alicia's father. During that time very little gave her pleasure, but her grandchildren provided some happiness and filled some empty hours. She knew she might be perceived as unfair, but she was living her life differently now. Yes, she had a man in her life, and she intended to enjoy these years. Sure, she would help out in an emergency, but for the most part, her schedule was packed.

Elena might sound a bit selfish, but she was very confident about her position. She is a loving mother and grandmother, and the ties to her family are important. Still, she is loosening those ties and is concentrating on her own life. Elena had no intention of giving up her own plans. Alicia, equally sure about the "unfairness of it all," continues to raise the issue. What was once a close relationship has suffered as a result of this conflict.

Does this problem have a correct answer? Some grown children are like Alicia, and they take it for granted that their parents will always be available for various duties and will continue to make sacrifices for their children. Perhaps these were the overindulged children, who have not completely grown up. Others may assume that their supportive parents will do whatever they ask.

Times and people change, however. No group has changed more than that of retirement age people. These people, many of whom are grandparents, often live more active lives than their parents did at the same age. They may even be more active than they themselves were as younger people. Some are enjoying themselves for the first time. And why not? They put in their years of child rearing. Their children are now responsible adults. So they happily choose their own activities, not really giving much thought to the approval of others. The ties that bound them so tightly in the past may be too constricting as they go about creating their new lives.

If this sounds like a big shift, consider that the younger generation in our culture is free to do as it pleases, too. The idea of carrying on the parents' traditions or choosing a career to please the parents is no longer part of our culture. The generations do not view themselves as accountable to each other as they once did. It is no wonder that many retired parents do not feel an obligation to baby-sit or play a specific and predictable role with their grandchildren.

I realize, of course, that some grandparents do, for many reasons, raise their grandchildren or play a pivotal role in their lives. This unique group may spend as much—or even more—time with the children as do the parents. Many young parents freely admit that having a grandparent provide daycare was a gift that has no adequate price tag. Today's family situations are nothing if not complex. We are, quite literally, making it up as we go along.

Who Loves Whom the Most?

Marion came to me for help with a situation she believed

was harming her children. Grandma Joyce seemed to love one of the three children more than the other two. Jon, the favored child, wasn't yet aware that he was favored, but the two girls wondered why Grandma hugged and kissed Jon so much more. They wondered why Grandma Joyce plays with Jon more and always "tells him how good he is."

When Marion asked her mother-in-law not to show this favoritism, she vehemently denied that she did such a thing. Yet, her special attention to Jon continued to be obvious to others in the family. When she was confronted again, she admitted that Jon reminded her of Billy, the son she had lost years ago.

We don't like to admit it, but we can have a special feeling about a particular child. If a grandparent—or a parent—is aware of this feeling, he or she must make every effort not to act on it or show it. Showing favoritism is destructive in families, just as it is in classrooms.

Parents may be able to protect their children from overt favoritism when they are small, but eventually it can be hurtful if not controlled. For example, Mel continuously talked about his grandson "the doctor" and never said a word about his other grandson, whom he didn't consider as accomplished. Jerilyn talked about Josh and Camryn but never mentioned Carol and Karl, her son-in-law's twins that her daughter is now helping him raise. Some reasons for favoritism may be deep and even painful, like Joyce's, but these issues must be resolved to avoid harming the children. Grandparents, like parents, are often called upon to alter their needs in order to do what is best for the children.

Shifting Loyalties

I have seen unequal attention and love result in angry, bitter feelings. Ultimately, the grandchildren's parents will protect them from potentially harmful behavior. If we are thinking clearly, we will admire the parents for stepping in and objecting when *anyone's* behavior is destructive to their children. After all, didn't we raise them to be responsible?

RELATIONSHIPS between grandchildren and grandparents change and shift with the times. For example, the grandparents who bring the most presents might indeed be "favored" by young children. As the years pass, the children may feel the strings that are attached to those presents (the strings really are there), or they may realize that their other grandparents didn't have the resources to be so generous or that they have different values and believe in modest gifts. The children may well come to feel more comfortable with the quieter love of these grandparents. Grandchildren's affections may shift many times throughout the years. When we gaze lovingly at these delightful creatures as they play with their first rattles, we can't predict what our relationships with them will be like. We can only offer our love to them and our support to their parents.

My Kids Are More Special, Aren't They Mom?

It isn't surprising that sibling rivalry continues even after the children have children. New opportunities to compete abound! Lynn keeps a mental scorecard, always totaling up her children's accomplishments and weighing them against her sister's children's. Then she tries to get her mother to agree that her children really are superior. Furthermore, she gets furious if her mother mentions one of her sister's children's accomplishments. What makes Lynn even more angry is the fact that Pamela, her sister, won't concede that Lynn's children really are better looking, smarter, and more accomplished. Pamela has learned to deal with her sister by not playing the game. She avoids engaging in these contests. Their mother and father won't play either, but Lynn continues to push, hoping—apparently—for a showdown over whose children are "better." How ridiculous, you think. Yes, but too often, the family dramas continue long after the children are grown and gone. In this family, one person has a very narcissistic need to be first in every way. It's actually very sad.

What's That in Her Nose?

Your precious, sweet, always well-behaved grandson turns twelve, and suddenly he sulks and barely nods at you. What's the matter with the parents? Why do they let him be rude to you? If that isn't bad enough your sixteen-year-old granddaughter comes to visit you and you see something in her nose—is that a ring? Are her parents crazy—have they lost their minds? She actually has a nose ring. Worse, you learn that the fifteen-year-old—the one you secretly loved best—has been suspended from school for smoking marijuana. Nothing to do but wash your hands of the whole mess. If only you had spoken up, you think. You could have done a much better job with these kids, who are now just a bunch of renegades.

One day, if you are fortunate to live a long life, your grandchildren will pass through the childhood years and enter adolescence. Their parents may be struggling and worried as they see their formerly easygoing children become difficult or even get into trouble. For grandparents this is a delicate time.

Your children may never need your support more than they do when their children are having problems.

I Wish She'd Love Him Now

Lou is very upset with his mother. For years she doted on Jud. According to Callie, her little Jud could do no wrong. What a polite boy—and so smart and handsome. Too bad her grandson had to grow up. Now, at fourteen, he's surly and his grades have dropped. Lou and Berta took him to counseling, but Callie believes that all Jud needs is a good talking-to. Callie told Lou that she didn't want to see Jud until he was straightened out! She actually believed her threat was going to make a difference in the family's problems. As it turned out, Callie never saw Jud again. He committed suicide. Lou and Berta not only have the grief and guilt to work through, they also have the memory of the sharp words of a once-doting grandmother who had, from their point of view, turned on Jud when he started having trouble. Of course, they also feel that Callie abandoned them, as well, when they most needed her support.

Grandparenting always looks like fun, and when the children are small, the problems usually seem small, too. Unfortunately, some grandparents withdraw when the going gets rough, and they often blame the parents. I've even seen grandparents show disapproval when a three-year-old is having a tantrum. They are so enthralled with being grandparents that they forget that the grandchildren will go through the normal stages of childhood, stages that can be very difficult. Some grandparents refuse to acknowledge that childhood is sometimes painful, and the children can be troubled.

In the early years, every parent and grandparent has fantasies about a perfect childhood. But no childhood is perfect. Over the years children go through many difficult stages. One child may have a learning disability; another may have severe physical problems; another might be shy and have difficulty making friends; another seems to have a penchant for getting into trouble. One client told me that she felt so much tension around her in-laws because they expected only perfection from the children. They didn't want to hear about a failing grade in math or a sleep problem or any difficulty at all. When the kids were young, it was easier to keep up the myths, but now that they were entering adolescence, it was becoming very hard to maintain the fiction of perfection. "Their son had been a very troubled teenager," the daughter-in-law said, "so I don't understand how they could expect this perfection from his children." The unrealistic expectations of these grandparents actually undermine the parents and make their job more difficult. Sometimes the parents are undermined in other ways. Some grandparents just won't say no.

I'll Call Grandma

Emily has wonderful memories of the visits to her grandparents. As an only child, she felt very special to have grandparents who loved her so deeply. They also gave her anything she wanted. If her parents refused to buy her something she wanted, she could just call Grandma Pauline, and her request was granted. (A virtual fairy godmother!)

Now that Emily is seventeen, she is lucky that she can turn to Pauline for advice and support. She especially likes to talk to Pauline when she is having a disagreement with her parents, Sid and Beth. Emily knows that Pauline will take her side and even try to persuade her parents to give in. Pauline always defends her granddaughter and at times has been harsh in her disagreements with Sid and Beth. The problems here are escalating, and unfortunately, Pauline does not have the good sense to stop overruling the parents. Sid and Beth's wishes for their child are being severely undermined. The resentments will last a long time.

The Circle Is Complete

Life expectancy being what it is, many grandchildren will become adults and still have living grandparents. The dreaded adolescence is over, and these once babbling darlings in a highchair are now going off to college, starting careers, and even getting married. This can be a wonderful stage for grandparents. A shift in the relationship that often starts when the children are in their teens is now permanent.

For years Grandma Hannah and Grandpa Leonard doted on the three grandkids, Zoe, Art, and Martha. They remembered every birthday, and holidays were fine affairs. But when these children reached their teens, their parents began to remind them to buy birthday cards for the grandparents. "It's your job to remember their needs now," their mother would say. "They poured so much attention on you, and they have done all the giving. It's your turn now," their father said. For a few years these children needed reminding and some nagging, but eventually, they began to initiate the calls and visits to the grandparents. The roles changed, and the former receivers were now the givers.

Hanging in with the eldest, Zoe, wasn't always easy for her parents or her grandparents. She was a troubled and rebellious girl who had once dyed her hair green and sported black lipstick and nails (the more mild of her rebellious acts). Hannah and Leonard loved her anyway and took her to their favorite restaurants and proudly introduced her to their friends (many of whom were most disapproving). It wasn't easy, but they took the long view, and Zoe the history professor is getting married next month. How wonderful!

The circle of unconditional love and caring is complete in this family. It is a reward based on sound decisions throughout the years these children were raised. I have watched it happen in many families. It is indeed rewarding for all three generations.

121

How Important Are These Ties?

Grandparents and grandchildren who have a loving, close relationship are very lucky, and the love they share is special. The difference in age and generational experience creates a unique opportunity to see issues from a different point of view. For grandparents, the love for these children is unconditional and unburdened by the demands and pressures of parenthood.

As for grandchildren, whose parents may be busy and preoccupied with the demands of providing for a family, the grandparent relationship may mean undivided time and attention from adults they adore. I've heard of grandparents who learned computer basics and got e-mail addresses just so they could communicate with their grandchildren, for whom computers are part of everyday life. The phone calls and letters, and of course, visits, are unlike those in any other relationship.

Naturally, this special bond must be encouraged and nurtured. Harmonious relationships between family members provide the best atmosphere in which this nurturing can take place. Below are suggestions to create and maintain harmony.

For the couple:

1. **Think about how much time you want your children to spend with their grandparents.** Then establish guidelines based on your decision.

2. **Be generous as you form your guidelines.** Remember, grandparents may love your children more than anyone else except you.

3. **Don't take advantage of grandparents.** They are not built in baby-sitters, and they aren't loan companies either. Even wealthy grandparents should not be expected to pay

your children's school tuition or summer camp fees. Respect your parents and in-laws' right to their own lives.

4. **Recognize that most grandparents do not fit the stereotype of doddering old folks.** Your parents have careers and interests and lives that may be very full without grandchildren. Do not expect them to suddenly start baking cookies or knitting little sweaters for grandkids. They are more likely to take them to the office to visit for an afternoon!

5. **Listen to grandparents' advice.** They may really know better than you. After all, they raised you. If you think that they made some big mistakes, and you don't want their advice, be gentle when you tell them to back off.

6. **Let them spoil the children a little.** You need to set limits, but a moderate amount of spoiling can't hurt. You can choose the areas in which the kids may or may not be "indulged." For example, if you are a vegetarian household, you have the right to insist that your children's diet be respected.

7. **Grandparents are individuals.** Do not compare what one set of grandparents does with and for the children with the other set. In-law relationships are complex enough without dividing the grandparents into armed camps.

8. **Expect and be grateful for the fact that your parents love all their grandchildren and will not love your children more.** Don't try to divide grandparents' loyalties with your own sibling rivalries.

9. **Nourish and encourage the grandparent tie.** These older adults have so much to offer. Your children will receive unlimited love, and they will also learn a great deal about giving love back. Don't cheat your children of this valuable relationship.

For the grandparents:

1. **Set limits on the time you spend with your grandchildren.** You have earned your free time. Make a life of your own—that's what your children have done and your grandchildren are learning to do.

2. Be generous, but set limits. Don't wait to have them set for you. Ask your children about their preferences. Remember, too, that if you bring a gift every time you visit, the children may begin to look forward to the gift more than to their time with you.

3. **Baby-sit and help out if you can.** You enjoyed time away from your children, and now your grown-up kids may need some time away too. If you can give this freely, then do it, but do not be a martyr about this. If it is too much to handle, then say so. Older grandparents may find baby-sitting physically taxing and have the right—indeed the obligation—to refuse this burdensome task.

4. **Don't give unsolicited advice.** You can make suggestions, but do not insist that your way is the only way, and keep criticism of the parents to yourself. Criticism of your own children is not ordinarily well accepted, and criticism of your in-law children is really foolish.

5. **Never overrule parents or do things without their permission.** They have the right to choose the children's religion, diet, clothing style, haircuts, and so on. (I once heard a story about a grandmother who, without permission, had her four-year-old granddaughter's long hair cut off. Needless to say, the parents were most unhappy.) If you believe something is really wrong with the care your grandchild is getting, then seek outside advice.

6. **Avoid becoming involved in unresolved sibling rivalry.** Let your children fight out their own problems, especially

if they are involving the grandkids in the rivalry.

7. **Hang in during the tough times.** These children aren't here only as a source of joy for you. Your grandchildren must make their way in a complex world. As they grow up, problems are bound to occur, some minor, some serious. Your children need your support when problems arise, especially serious concerns. Grandparents should be a nonjudgmental support system for both their children and grandchildren.

8. **Be accepting of all the children and do not have excessive fantasies about how many grandchildren you "should" have.** The trend today is for smaller families. Your children do not need pressure to produce more children because you want them.

9. **Nourish and encourage the relationships.** You want the tie to last even if the parents divorce or they move to the Alaskan wilds. Be prepared for change, but nurture the relationship over the years.

Every Family Is Different

The above guidelines and suggestions are flexible in that they can be adapted to any family situation. All family members benefit from close, warm ties with extended family members. But as we all know, life changes. What was once a stable family unit might become a family in crisis, with divorce being considered. Given the divorce rate we have today, is it any wonder that in-law relationships can become strained? In the next chapter, we'll explore what can happen when the ties that bind are broken.

6 WHEN THE TIES UNRAVEL

*M**arriage* is forever. Well, it's forever in theory and in fairy tales, but about half the time in our society, it turns out not to be a permanent commitment. Some people believe that many couples stand at the altar with the idea that they will divorce if "things just don't work out." From my experience, this is not the case. Most couples do plan to make their marriage last, and they promise each other that they will work hard to resolve differences. If they don't give up too soon (which may mean seeking marriage counseling when troubles crop up), and if they are lucky, they may reap the rewards of a lifelong, satisfying marriage.

Unfortunately, in spite of happy beginnings and good intentions, many relationships do not stand the test of time, and a divorce results. On the other hand, some marriages don't stand the test of time but rather than divorcing, the couple stays together out of social or family pressures or perhaps because they are too frightened to go it alone. These are the empty and rather sad marriages in which the partners have little regard for each other. They merely tolerate each other's presence and share their finances, their home, and perhaps relationships with children and grandchildren.

While we talk a considerable amount about marriages "failing," we should probably put some attention on the sham marriages that are unfortunately so common. There is no right or wrong answer about whether to end a marriage. I have worked with clients who made the decision to stay married because they enjoyed many aspects of their life and the benefits that came from being married. I have also worked with clients who found that type of "arrangement" intolerable and ended their marriages. Either way, it is up to the individuals involved, and no one can decide what is right for another person. In this, as in so many areas of life, it is important to follow one's own heart.

The Dreaded Divorce

For those who end their marriages through divorce, the reality is that they will experience anxiety, stress, and all manner of emotional pain. It may take many years to recover from the trauma of divorce. A minority of men and women never completely get over the turmoil and emotional damage and carry the scars with them throughout their lives. Some people are more resilient, or perhaps they were more clear about the decision to divorce, and they move forward with their lives, perhaps even maintaining—or mending—relationships with the in-law family.

The Long Path to Healing

In my counseling practice I see many individuals, families, couples, and children who have been unable to handle the trauma involved in divorce. Some come for therapy before or during the divorce, but some may seek help long after the final divorce decree. I have observed emotions ranging from despair and depression to anger, bitterness, and intense hatred, often with a deep desire for revenge.

The children of divorce may believe the divorce is their fault; even years after the divorce, they may blame themselves for their parents' breakup. Needless to say, many young people in this situation feel guilty and confused, and the whole family suffers.

I Don't Recognize Myself!

I think of Lewis with sadness. When I first met him I was immediately struck by his quiet, gentle manner. In tears, he told me that he couldn't get over the fact that his wife had left him. And they had had a good marriage—better than most, he observed. Or so he thought. For many years he believed in what he saw as a stable, loving relationship. Naturally, he was hurt and humiliated when one night he found a note telling him that she had moved in with Rob, who had a been friend to both of them.

Lewis just couldn't shake his loneliness and deep sadness. Rather than feeling angry toward Natalie, which I assured him would be normal, he insisted that he loved her dearly, and he turned the blame on himself. He must have done *something* wrong. (Many men and women do this. They spend many months and perhaps years trying to figure out the one thing they did wrong that resulted in the divorce.)

One day Lewis came into my office with a surprising story. The previous evening he had gone to Natalie's new house, hoping to just catch a glimpse of her. He didn't see her, but he did see the car they had picked out together. Lewis was overcome with sadness as he remembered the fun they had had deciding on the model and the color. But then he began to get mad. How could she do this? His anger was turning to rage as he thought about the way she had left him. He had rushed up to the car and started pounding the hood. It didn't stop there, however. Next he broke off the windshield wipers, and then he smashed the windshield! Last, but not least, he had slashed the tires with his penknife.

This level of violence from a gentle, quiet man? Yes, Lewis, who had refused to face his anger, eventually engaged in this kind of irrational, vengeful behavior. I could give examples of many more individuals for whom the trauma of divorce led to behavior that at one time they would not have believed was part of their character. For instance, Mimi held up fairly well during the many months the divorce battle raged on between the lawyers, but once the final papers were in her hands, she went to bed and did not get up for days. It was a long time before this usually upbeat and energetic woman was again functioning normally. In other examples, Arthur missed his wife and children so much that he started using alcohol and drugs to dull his pain, while Joan began to harass her ex-husband with hysterical phone calls. When she discovered that he had a woman friend, she threatened to kill her.

This is how traumatic divorce can be. But the majority of people, even Lewis, Mimi, Arthur, and Joan, eventually pick up the pieces and move on. If these unhappy individuals are lucky enough to have friends and family who are loving and supportive, they usually recover more quickly and are able to manage the bad times better. This may be a time when family members who were not welcomed with open arms before are leaned upon now. Parents may support their adult children, and grandparents may offer grandchildren a refuge from the storm of warring parents. Sometimes, however, parents are involved *before* an actual divorce occurs.

It's All Your Mother's Fault

After just three years of marriage, Susan and Bruce are close to calling the lawyers and starting divorce proceedings. They came to see me for counseling because they decided to make one last-ditch attempt to save their marriage. Over the telephone, Susan told me that she didn't want a divorce, but she could no longer live with her husband's and her in-laws' constant criticism.

During our first session, Bruce and Susan were both eager to explain why they could no longer live together. Bruce began by telling me that his parents had been right when they had warned him about Susan's strong will and stubborn ways. When they had first met her, they said they knew she would be unpleasant to live with because she was just too set in her ways. They had tried to convince their son to break off his relationship with her and find another woman, one who wouldn't be so intent on "doing her own thing." "I should have listened," Bruce said. "Susan is so strong willed it is impossible to change her mind once she makes a decision."

Susan glared at her husband, but she agreed that she had a tendency to be stubborn. She also admitted that she had strong opinions that were tough to change. She even acknowledged that she was used to getting her own way. Susan then said, "I love Bruce, and I know I must learn to compromise on many issues. But I would give in much more easily if I knew I was giving in to Bruce and not to his parents, too." Very interesting.

This is a profound statement, actually, and its implications became the focus of numerous counseling sessions. Susan was well aware that her in-laws did not like her— that was obvious from the day they had met her. What she found most unbearable was Bruce's habit of discussing their areas of disagreement with his parents. "Aren't these private things?" Susan asked. This situation was made even worse because Bruce would then "share" his parents' opinions with Susan. They always sided with him, of course, and he even included their unflattering comments about her. Their smug "I-told-you-so" attitude signaled the end of the road for Susan.

Susan and Bruce have very different temperaments and personalities. They were also raised in different environments, and the ideas and opinions that had been ingrained during their childhood years were worlds apart. No wonder they had trouble compromising today. An important goal of counseling was to help them gain an understanding of their differences and, in addition, to respect and accept differences. Once they reached a willingness to be more accepting of each other, they could see that it was possible to incorporate both sets of ideas into their life together.

To reach this stage, it was critical that the "third-party" criticism of Susan that was so devastating to the marriage be removed. The "I-told-you-so" attitude aggravated an already bad situation. The goal was to reach a deeper understanding of each other and improve communication. If Bruce could disregard his parents' negative opinions of his wife—and keep them quiet—then Susan was less likely to be so stubborn.

Too Close for Comfort

In evaluating this couple, I considered it clear that Bruce was closely tied to his parents. At his stage of life, he should not have been running to them every time he had an argument with his wife. Unfortunately for Susan, he had never made the normal transition to full adulthood. Had he done this, he would have automatically resolved issues and problems on his own. Bruce's parents encouraged his dependency, which deepened it further. In some families, the children must be nudged to leave the nest. To Bruce's credit, he had defied his parents when he fell head over heels for Susan. He had been uncomfortable with their disapproval but had thought they would eventually come around. As a matter of fact, Bruce wanted his parents' approval so badly, he tried to make sure it would happen by insisting that Susan conform! Unfortunately, this reaction is very common, if often unconscious.

So who is the cause of this faltering marriage? Should we blame Bruce or his parents? Perhaps Susan is to blame because she won't change to please the other three people she is "married" to. Frankly, it would be easy to blame the critical, overbearing in-laws. However, the criticism they lobbed toward Susan would have stopped if Bruce had refused to listen to it. *The parents-in-law interfered because they were allowed to.*

The real work to rebuild this marriage began when Bruce and Susan agreed to resolve their issues in counseling and without interference from Bruce's parents. This was difficult, because Bruce's parents were angry and hurt. They were reluctant to let go, and Bruce had to make the break alone—with Susan's support.

In counseling, Bruce had to work on his feelings of guilt about separating from his parents. Susan had a difficult time of it because she had been blaming all her negative behavior on her in-laws. Now she had to deal with her own demons, and she did indeed have "an attitude," as the kids today say. This was going to be a long process—and hard work was ahead—but at least they were on the right track.

Would this marriage have been salvageable if the criticism had gone on ten, twenty, or forty years? It is impossible to say for sure, but I believe Susan and Bruce had a better chance of making a go of the marriage because they caught the problem relatively early, and they agreed to seek counseling. In addition, their individual problems were going to hold them back in life. For example, Bruce's dependence on the opinion of his parents was similarly played out in his work. He was always looking for approval from his boss, often to the point of seeming immature and needy. Susan's stubborn streak caused her trouble with those she supervised. She wouldn't admit a mistake if it killed her. Seeking marriage counseling can bring benefits beyond repairing a marriage.

Am I Ready for This Step?

Marriages generally have a greater chance to succeed if individuals have had some experience leading independent lives before they marry. This time of independence allows the young adult to separate from the family of origin. One of Bruce's difficulties was the fact that he really didn't know how to take care of his own needs without his parents' help. The result was this unhealthy dependency, not just on his parents, but on other people generally. It is one thing to want parental approval; it is quite another thing to be miserable without it. A period of independence can foster the normal separation from parents that is necessary to form a healthy marriage bond in our society.

Go Fight Your Own Battles

Mel and Lydia were much like Susan and Bruce. They had difficulty making their own decisions. Both Mel and Lydia asked everyone else, especially their parents, to help them make choices. Long before they became engaged, they recognized their many differences, most of which they were unable to resolve. The one decision they made, however, was to get married. At least they agreed on that!

The arguments went on and on, before the wedding, after the wedding, and even during holiday dinners with their families. One Thanksgiving, they had dinner with both sets of parents and spent the day asking for help to mediate their argument. If only the parents had had the good sense to stay out of it. But they didn't. Lydia's parents were particularly opinionated, not to mention quite insensitive. Mel was most unhappy to hear their comments or take their advice. Of course, Lydia thought the advice Mel's parents happily—and quite politely—offered was pretty lousy.

Mel and Lydia continued their bickering and carrying on for many years, with all four parents willing to jump in. (They probably spent all their holidays together because no one else wanted them around!) The dynamic changed when Mel was transferred across the country to San Francisco and the couple didn't have their parents handy. They lasted about six months, and then Lydia packed up and moved back "home" to the East Coast. Without the in-laws around to squabble over, Mel and Lydia had nothing to talk—or argue—about. Mel and Lydia were not ready for the "big step" of marriage, regardless of their age.

Allowed to Interfere—The Crucial Phrase

Am I saying that parents should never give advice to their grown children? No, that is not the point. We all need ideas and opinions from other people, friends as well as family. I'm not suggesting that a couple is an island, with no means of transportation to get on or off. Rather, each couple is an island with ferry service and an airport. As long as each member of the couple and all the in-law parents recognize that all parties must make their own decisions, advice can be helpful.

PARTNERS will usually find something on which to blame their relationship problems, and sometimes in-laws make good targets. And without doubt, some in-laws do create problems in a marriage, but only if they are *allowed to interfere*. The magic phrase applies.

Each partner has an obligation to stop criticism of the other partner and not allow parents to participate in decisions that are private matters between the couple. If the partner is unable to separate in this way, then he or she is probably too immature for marriage. Marriage ties do not unravel because of in-laws; these ties unravel because couples allow in-laws to interfere, and for whatever reason, because couples refuse to work on their problems as a team, independent from other family members.

Making a Bad Situation Worse

When a divorce occurs, the best possible scenario for each partner is the support of a loving family. When parents, and sometimes siblings, too, heap on blame and criticism, they only make things worse. I have seen this too many times. A bossy sister says, "I always knew he was a jerk, and now I'm proved right," to her younger sister, who just separated from her husband of twenty years. Or a mother says, "You never could stick to anything, and I told you that we do not approve of divorce in our family." (That's always a helpful remark.)

My clients often remark about the gratitude they feel toward parents and in-laws for their support during the difficult period of separation and divorce. Perhaps the best thing siblings and parents can do is to offer to listen if the person would like to talk but to refrain from jumping in with criticism of the former in-law. People say many things when they are distraught, and it is not wise to go on record having agreed that the former in-law child is a low-down, dirty dog. Particularly when children are involved, it is important not to paint too negative a picture of one of the parents.

How Can In-Laws Help?

Margaret got along quite well with her in-laws, Will and Lois, perhaps because during fourteen years of marriage, she saw them only at family events and had made no efforts to extend contact beyond these obligatory gatherings. The children visited their grandparents often, usually with their dad, Ted.

After four weeks of living without Ted, who had moved out and filed for divorce, Margaret was at the end of her rope. The stress of taking care of the house and the kids by herself was proving too much for her during this unhappy time. More than once she thought she might "lose it." She was either too depressed to be a patient and attentive mother or she was so irritable all she could do was yell. After a month of handling it all alone, Margaret began to rethink her relationship with Will and Lois.

One evening, desperate and feeling helpless, Margaret called her in-laws, and through her tears she pleaded for their help. Lois and Will dearly loved their grandchildren and quickly offered support. When Lois had first learned about her son's impending divorce, she had feared that she would see less of her beloved grandchildren. She and Will had been puzzled and hurt by their daughter-in-law's distant attitude, and they wished they had been invited to visit more often. Now that they were given the opportunity to help, they willingly became more involved with their grandchildren.

Margaret and Ted's children were unhappy and confused by their parents' divorce. Although they had been aware that little warmth moved between their parents, they never expected that their family would fall apart. Now they missed their dad and felt abandoned by him. Their mother's erratic moods, the intermittent sadness followed by extreme anger and irritability, had them on edge much of the time. Like most children, they wondered if they had done something to make their parents angry enough to separate.

Unfortunately, Margaret, who had the primary care of the children, was unprepared for a divorce. Her emotional devastation required professional help and time to heal, and her in-laws were able to rise to the occasion to help out with the children. In the midst of chaos, the three children could count on some stability in their lives.

Will and Lois made no attempt to interfere in their son's divorce. The fact is, they weren't that close to Ted either, and they didn't know why the marriage broke up. They resolved that it was none of their business. Since the grandparents bore no animosity toward the parents, the children could feel more secure, and the grandparents could reassure the children that this period of trauma would one day be over. Their mother would regain her equilibrium, and they would continue to see their father and their grandparents. The children had an opportunity to adjust to a great change in their lives with the help of two supportive grandparents.

When Help Is Not on the Way

In-laws may choose not to become involved or they may become involved in a non-supportive or even destructive way. Even the grandparent role may be disrupted during a divorce. I have heard many explanations for this behavior. In a therapy session, parents may bitterly blame the in-law child for the divorce, or they are angry at their own child and choose to withdraw. Sometimes parents understand that their child is more to blame—divorce is not always a fifty-fifty proposition. Of course, they may or may not be right.

Shelly was angry with her son for (as she succinctly put it) screwing around on his wife. "She finally threw him out," Shelly said, "and I'm glad she did. The truth is, Robin is too good for my son." Frannie was angry at her daughter for bringing "shame" to the family by divorcing a man who was not only a "good provider" but who appeared to be a "pillar of the community." (No matter that "upstanding" Jake was addicted to pornography and spent *every* evening locked in the basement with these movies. He even slept in his basement "hideaway.")

Some grandparents have told me that they are just too busy to help out, and they don't want the burden of becoming too involved in their children's lives. Frankly, I've seen some parents/grandparents who are just too selfish and uncaring to offer any support. For example, Tanya told her distraught daughter, "You made your bed, now lie in it. Don't bother me—you're raised, and I'm not raising your kids, too." (Tanya had asked if her children could visit for a weekend while she found a new apartment, one she could afford.) Fortunately, this kind of attitude is relatively rare. It is one thing to hold children responsible for their own lives; it is another thing to turn away from them and have no compassion at all.

Loving to Help—and Hurt

Georgia never liked Sam, her daughter's ex-husband. Sam wasn't too fond of Georgia either. Now that Sam and Ellen are divorced, Georgia thinks she is free to express her real feelings, and so she does—frequently! "Sam is a no-good bum," she says. "His family is so low class—you're so much better off without him. Didn't I tell you not to marry such a loser?"

These opinions do not bother Ellen very much. She is hurt because this "low-class loser bum" cheated on her with a succession of women. But, as a protective mother, Ellen believes it is not healthy for her children to hear this kind of talk about their father, especially from their grandmother. Regardless of her own anger and pain, Ellen knows that it's best that the children maintain a loving relationship with their dad. As a child of divorce herself, Ellen understands her children's predicament and has resolved that her children have the benefit of two loving parents who do not snipe at each other. Sam understands that his inability to be sexually faithful has led to the divorce, and he is not criticizing Ellen—no matter what!

Is This Support or Vindictiveness?

It is common for friends and relatives to choose up sides when a divorce is in the works. Well-meaning as it may be, it may lead to hurt feelings, at the very least, and a permanent wound in the relationship at worst. Grandma Georgia must be stopped. She is at risk of being kept away from her grandchildren; Ellen feels that strongly about the destructive nature of Georgia's endless criticism of Sam.

▬▬▬

ONE of the worst situations imaginable occurs when children feel that they must choose sides. They get this message because of the opinions they hear from others. Being told how "bad" the other parent is creates more confusion. While the children may be angry at the parent who appears to be the "cause" or perpetrator of the divorce, it is in their best interest to continue to love both parents.

▬▬▬

I'm Divorcing All Three of You!

Like Will and Lois, Leo and Judy wanted to help their grand-children heal after their family's breakup. They couldn't bear to see how hard these children were taking their parents' divorce. For the sake of the children, Leo and Judy were willing to be nonjudgmental and set aside their own feelings about their former daughter-in-law, Lori. Lori, however, was bitter and angry at her former husband and decided to cut all ties to his family. Tragically, that included Leo and Judy.

When I met Judy and Leo, they were depressed as well as frustrated. They believed they had lost their grandchildren, and they desperately missed the close relationship they had had with these much-adored children. As a result of the divorce agreement their son had signed with Lori, they were rarely permitted to see the three kids. This was a terrible blow. When the parents first separated, Leo and Judy assumed that they would be able to pick up the kids and spend the day at the zoo or amusement park or at their house, where they had special games and videos for the kids. They had been doing this for years, so why would it stop just because their son had left the home? They were shocked when Lori told them that these regular visits were over. She told them they were a "bad influence" on the children, and therefore, she was drastically limiting the time they could spend with Leo and Judy.

Leo and Judy's visits are now timed to coincide with their son's twice-monthly visitation. But Jeff wants to spend some private time with his children, so they see the grandkids only for a few hours every other week. This situation is made worse because Leo and Judy believe that Lori's vindictive-ness is the cause of all this trouble. They don't necessarily blame her for the divorce, but they do blame her for divorc-ing them and establishing unreasonable rules for their relationship with the kids. If she wants to punish Jeff, they wish she would find a way that doesn't involve them.

Jeff has always been quite close to his parents, and it hurts him to see them victimized this way. He doesn't like his children given negative messages either. A few months after the divorce, Jeff went to Lori and asked her to consider allowing the children to be with his parents more frequently. Lori just laughed, however, and reminded him that he had agreed to limited custody, and she had the signed papers to prove it. She was under no obligation to arrange special time with *his* parents.

The next week Jeff tried again. This time he appealed to Lori to consider how hard it was for the children to lose their grandparents during this already stressful time. And wouldn't they end up blaming her for their inability to spend time with Judy and Leo? This time Lori bitterly reminded Jeff that any break in the relationship between his parents and the children was his fault because the divorce was his idea.

It was clear that Lori would extract her revenge any way she could. Jeff would pay, and Leo and Judy would pay, too. They would continue to have only limited access to these precious children. Lori was not ready to see that the three kids were being made to pay too. In my practice, I have often been surprised by how frequently parents, most of whom ordinarily are quite sensible, resort to revenge against their former spouse and the in-law family. They may know their behavior is harming the children, but they can't help themselves.

Lori used the most ridiculous reasons to justify her behavior. "Leo and Judy eat too much junk food and let the kids stay up too late," she says. "They watch sitcoms, and they don't read enough," she adds. Therefore, she concludes, they will ruin her children's lives. This is enough to make a person cry. Yet, until she "sees the light," she cannot be forced to change.

There Ought to Be a Law

Because some grandparents have decided to take legal action to demand visitation rights, a few states now have laws that protect grandparents' relationships with grandchildren. These states have recognized an injustice and sought to remedy it. This is a delicate area, however, because it does interfere with the primary rights of parents, and it opens up another area for litigation in a court system that is already overloaded. The best remedy is to prevent these needless acts of revenge. Leo and Judy's situation was made worse because Lori's mother and siblings took her side and egged her on. They were confusing an offer of emotional support with agreeing with a destructive decision. This would have been the time when a gentle reminder that Lori was hurting her children was in order. "Getting behind" a person does not mean condoning vengeful acts.

But We Like the Guy!

Marla and Gordon were thrilled when Samantha married Roger, and over the years they had grown to love him like a son. Roger, Samantha, and their two kids spent a lot of time with Marla and Gordon, so they were saddened when they learned that the couple had separated. The in-laws immediately called Roger and told him that they wanted to maintain a close relationship with him. They were disappointed that the family atmosphere would change, but they could accept that as long as Roger stayed part of their lives. Samantha was all for this family harmony, so the situation looked ideal.

For about a year this happy "broken" family setup worked just fine. Marla and Gordon invited Roger over for dinner with the kids, and he invited them to his new apartment. Samantha and Roger celebrated the kids' birthdays together with Gordon and Marla—and Roger's parents too. But before long, Roger started dating, and his Saturday nights were no longer free to spend with his former in-laws. Marla and Gordon were not pleased that he was popular with "other" women, and it wasn't long before they were openly critical of his new "lifestyle," as they called it. They complained about his less-frequent visits, and they were most upset when he told them that he was developing serious feelings about a woman he was dating. The visits soon became strained, and eventually they stopped altogether.

The mistake that Marla, Gordon, and Roger made was assuming that they could go on as before. They tried to pretend that because they all loved each other, nothing would change. At first their situation seemed "ideal," which is rare when divorce is involved. Inevitably, though, the ties began to loosen. From what I have observed, it is impossible to maintain the same relationship with in-law family members when the marital bond breaks. This is sad, because it may mean that individuals who care about each find that their ties unravel. Rarely can it be any other way.

This is not to say that relationships can't remain cordial and even loving on some level. Ariel was fond of her daughter-in-law, Starr, and thought of her as the daughter she never had. Frankly, she couldn't fault Starr when she divorced Barney. Her son refused to seek help for his problems, which had made the marriage untenable. Starr was grateful for the support Ariel freely gave her. In fact, Ariel was so generous that Starr sometimes worried that she was giving too much to her and to the children. Furthermore, Starr, who was eager to begin a new life, was not sure she could keep up the new role of "girlfriend" that Ariel seemed to expect.

Eventually, Starr pulled away from Ariel, which was to

be expected. Unfortunately, Ariel remained disappointed in Starr and interpreted her natural desire for a new life as a rejection. Over the years, the relationship remained cordial and affectionate, but it wasn't possible for these two former relatives to become girlfriends.

Another Day, Another Marriage

For those going through a divorce, it may seem as if normal life is gone, never to return. But one need only look around to see that not only does life go on, love might be better the second time around. At least hope springs eternal, and many men and women remarry. Second and even third marriages are commonplace, and oh my, here come some new in-laws.

The so-called blended family consists of the parents and some or all of each partner's children. This is the primary unit. The secondary unit includes the grandparents of all the children, who are now new in-law parents to the partners. And let's not forget the siblings. Sometimes, this "new blend" can be quite confusing, and no one is sure who among this group actually counts as relatives. The former in-laws are the kids' grandparents, but the new in-laws are step-grand-parents, and new bonds are forming all over the place.

I'll never forget May, who when asked how many grand-children she had, began counting on her fingers. "Well, I had nine, but then when my son divorced his second wife, she disappeared and took her two kids from a former marriage with her, so then I had seven. But then he remarried and that wife has one, so now I have eight. Of course, Les [her other son] and Sue are getting divorced, and I'll lose Sue's child from her first marriage, so I'll be down to seven again." Somehow, through it all, May managed to squeeze some fun out of the chaotic marriages and remarriages of her children. Each new child was happily welcomed, and the birthdays duly noted.

Closing Doors, Opening Doors, Revolving Doors

May's family situation ended up being a revolving door of new and old relationships. Most people, however, are forced to close one door and wait to see if another will open. This period can be very trying for all family members.

Vicky found herself in a very odd situation. When she saw her son's four children, they were very uninhibited about talking about their mother's new boyfriend. Farley was great! He took them out to dinner two or three nights a week. He helped them with their homework, and this great guy even helped their mom get settled in the new house. Just last night, he painted the living room! The kids were happy to see their mom happy and Farley sure was fun—and he has three boys of his own. The house was big and had plenty of room even when the boys visited.

All this enthusiasm put Vicky in a very odd position. Her former daughter-in-law, Gina, had moved on with her life, but her son, Aaron, clearly had not. Just last week, Aaron had told Vicky that he was planning to work toward a reconciliation with Gina. He talked about all the progress he was making in counseling. Poor Aaron was so optimistic about a future with Gina that it broke Vicky's heart. It was clear that Aaron knew nothing about this Farley fellow. The kids apparently hadn't mentioned him to their dad. So what should she do?

Obviously, Vicky had choices. First, she could do nothing. She could stay out of the whole thing and let the "chips fall," so to speak. Or she could tell her son about the way the kids were talking and gently prod him to go to Gina and ask her if she was interested in a reconciliation. Her third choice involved approaching Gina and asking her if she and Farley were serious. This was a risky choice, but Vicky took it. As it turned out, she was glad she did.

Gina, who was fond of Vicky, told her former mother-in-law that she was very serious about Farley, and in fact, she had told Aaron that she expected to remarry within the year. Apparently, Aaron refused to accept that their divorce was indeed a divorce. According to Gina, Aaron stopped by unannounced, and most of the time he ignored Farley. One night, Gina was forced to ask him to leave because they were all going to the movies. Aaron then said, "I'll take you and the kids to the movies. You can send that guy home." She was actually very worried about Aaron and was glad Vicky had called.

Vicky followed her own heart and took the risk to call Gina, and as a result, she learned that her son was in very bad shape. As the story unfolded, it turned out that he was not being forthright with his therapist, who was encouraging a reconciliation based on the "facts" Aaron presented.

Vicky followed her heart again when she confronted Aaron about his continuing state of denial. At first Aaron resisted and fought her, but after a few weeks, when Gina and Vicky talked to Aaron together, he saw that he had indeed been living in a fantasy world of his own making.

It was sad for Gina and Vicky to witness the minor "breakdown" Aaron had when he realized what he had been doing. I call this breakdown minor because it did not require hospitalization. It required an intense period of mourning to reach acceptance, and for a few months Aaron was quite fragile. I'm happy to say he has recovered and is building a new life. Meanwhile, Gina and Farley are adjusting to their blended family. Vicky's decisions remind us that most situations have more than one right answer. Her choice to approach her daughter-in-law was not based on a need to meddle. Rather, it was based on a hunch that her son was in trouble. I think she did the right thing to follow her hunch.

New Ties, New Problems

Annie was unhappily married for ten years. Her relationship with her mother-in-law was adversarial, too. No wonder Annie was happy to say good riddance to Ryan and his whole family. But now she is in love again and is considering marrying Nick. She had once joked to a friend that she'd only marry again if her new husband's mother was dead! But here was Mom Dara, alive and well, and Nick has already told Annie that he enjoys spending time with his family. So far, Dara has been most pleasant, but Annie has her doubts about this new beginning. Is trouble in store?

Karen is another new wife who is already having second-marriage in-law problems. Karen is planning a "sweet sixteen" party for Brittany, and her new husband, Steve, insists that his parents be invited. He wants to show them that they will always be welcome at family events. Still smarting over their son's divorce (after four years!), they are anticipating being alienated from their new daughter-in-law. This will probably be a self-fulfilling prophecy because they have already let Karen know that she can never replace their much-loved ex-daughter-in-law.

Of course Karen will invite her ex-husband and his parents to Brittany's party. She won't leave out these important people in Brittany's life. But Karen is nervous about facing her former in-laws. She knows they loathe her and blame her for the divorce. With all these in-laws and exes coming, Karen is now dreading a day she should be anticipating with joy in her heart. "Oh well," she says, "let's get this day over with and hope that not too many sparks fly."

David and Lila face yet another second-family in-law problem. Lila's children are miserable every time they must visit their stepfather's parents. They don't understand why they have to visit this new set of grandparents when they can barely find time to visit their "real" grandparents. And why can't their real grandparents take them on trips like they used to? And why do David's kids always have to come along? Why can't these new kids go places with their own grandparents? Both sets of grandparents are none too thrilled either. Why, they ask, is it necessary for everything to be so "equal," when it is clear it can't be. The atmosphere around this household is great fun! Arguing, sniping, and jealousy fill the air. I'm glad I don't have to go there for dinner. No wonder Lila and David are having problems. Second marriages have a high divorce rate; perhaps these kinds of issues tell us why.

Ty and Lena are an active couple in their mid-fifties. They have a daughter, Heather, who is in her twenties. She just left her husband after only eighteen months of marriage. Ty and Lena stayed out of it and considered it fortunate that Heather had no children. For years Ty and Lena played golf with the couple next door, Jodi and Tom. Then Jodi died, and Tom was despondent. Ty and Lena did everything they could to support him through his grief. They invited him to their backyard barbecues, and they still played golf as often as they could.

During one of her parents' patio parties, Heather spent quite a bit of time talking with Tom. Later that week, he called her, and much to her surprise, asked her to have dinner with him. One dinner led to another and another and soon, they were having breakfast together too. At first they kept their relationship a secret. "I can't even imagine what my parents would think," Heather said. Tom agreed.

One evening Ty and Lena stopped by Heather's new apartment to drop off a gift. And who should they find there—in his bathrobe, no less—but Tom. Awkward does not describe the scene. Eventually, after months of protests, tears, threats, and anguish, Tom became Ty and Lena's son-in-law. A year later, Tom became a dad, and his grown daughter had a child, too, so he was a dad for the third time and a grandfather for the first time, events that occurred in the same month. Tom's grown children thought it was strange to have a stepmother their own age, but they adjusted. Too bad Ty and Lena couldn't. They just can't accept that Heather would marry a man old enough to be her father, and they think that Tom is just a "dirty old man" who tricked her.

All these individuals provide examples of the kinds of problems that families create when they form, dissolve, and reconstitute themselves. The end of a marriage doesn't necessarily mean the end of ties, but the beginning of another marriage means that new ties are forming. And it can be a mess!

When Jealousy Takes Over

Enid is jealous of Rita, her husband's ex-wife. Gary has to talk to Rita quite often because they have three kids, but all this friendly communication is very upsetting. It's just as upsetting that Gary frequently talks to his former in-laws because the children spend so much time with them. He's always off picking up the kids from their house or he's consulting them about various plans they're making.

After almost every conversation Gary has with Rita or his ex-in-laws, he and Enid have a huge argument. This is unfortunate because Gary is a devoted father and calls his children almost every day. That means he talks with Rita almost every day too!

Is this one-year-old second marriage in trouble? You bet it is. During a counseling session I had with them, Gary explained that he loves his children and he wants to maintain a good relationship with the other people who love them too. And he admits that he is quite fond of his ex-in-laws and even enjoys their company. He doesn't want these ties to break completely. A couple of sessions later, Gary admits that he still has feelings for Rita! He continues to feel protective of and warm toward the mother of his children and the woman he lived with for twelve years. Is that so strange? But of course, he quickly adds, he is crazy about Enid. He wants to stay married to her.

Once this couple was in counseling for a while, it became easier for them to express their deepest feelings to each other. Enid was able to talk about how jealous she is of Rita and admit she is afraid that Gary is still in love with her. Enid was not "paranoid," as Gary once said, because she was threatened by Rita. Gary had to realize that his continuing ties to Rita and his former in-laws were playing a role in her jealousy. Her deepest fear was that he wanted to go back in time and restore the marriage he'd lost.

Fortunately, Enid and Gary are committed to counseling because they want their marriage to last. They express genuine love for each other, and I am very hopeful that they can understand what their feelings are all about. If they stick with it, a good chance exists that Enid's jealousy will gradually diminish and that Gary will be more "tuned in" to Enid's feelings.

George and Sandy came to my office and told their story

of jealousy and misunderstanding. This time it was the husband who was jealous. Sandy was a much-loved in-law child, and she and her former mother-in-law still get together often for dinner and an evening at the mall. Rob might be out of the picture, but his mother, Marilyn, is still part of Sandy's life. Actually, Marilyn was very protective of Sandy and furious with Rob for demanding a divorce. Now George is jealous of the time his new wife spends with Marilyn. This is his first marriage, and he thought he and Sandy would be best friends and spend almost all their time together. But to him, it seems that Marilyn is Sandy's best pal. Why would Sandy want to shop with Marilyn instead of spending an evening with him?

George has misinterpreted some of his wife's behavior. In his mind, her friendship with Marilyn means that she misses her old life—and good ol' Rob too. In essence, he is saying, "I think Sandy must be in love with Rob if she needs to spend so much time with his mother." The fact is, Sandy has many women friends and always has had a life independent of whomever she is married to! Fortunately, Sandy and George are in counseling, too. Once a week they have a safe place to talk openly about these confusing feelings.

Jealousy is a common emotion in family life, but it is even more common in second marriages, in part because of the close ties to a first family that may remain. Once again, we can see that it is often difficult to create distance from ties that bind.

The First Choice Was Better

According to Max and Monique, their son's first wife, Gloria, was "a living doll." They'll tell you that their former daughter-in-law was the perfect wife, and Richard's second wife, Jesse can never live up to the wonderful Gloria. She kept the cleanest house, gave the best parties, was an excellent mother, and took wonderful care of their son. (She probably worked on her doctoral dissertation and made thousands dabbling in stocks in her spare time, too.) Anyway, the list of Gloria's virtues was long, indeed—and Jesse knows every item on it because Max and Monique regularly talk about Gloria. Of course, it is difficult for Jesse to hear all this, but what hurts even more is that Richard doesn't say a word while his parents rave about his first wife.

It is possible that if Richard took a few suggestions to heart, things could immediately improve. First, he must tell his parents not to mention Gloria to his second wife. The topic of Gloria should be forbidden, end of story. Furthermore, he can tell them that he doesn't want to hear anymore about her either. He can even let them know they are mistaken about Gloria. In fact, when it comes to being a good wife, Jesse has Gloria beat by a mile. Richard can't control what his parents think or what they talk about when they're alone. But it is possible for him to intervene and prevent these hurtful remarks when Jesse is present. If they refuse to listen to Richard's suggestions, he can stop seeing them until they get the message.

It is always a puzzle why in-laws so often tend to like the first choice of a mate better. Could it be that they are critical individuals with a poor memory and they have chosen to forget the problems they had the first time around? Bootsie and Mort are another set of parents who think their daughter Barbara did much better with her first husband. They keep hoping that Barbara will rethink her current situation and leave Carter, her second husband. They think Carter is too "uptight" to be around their grandchildren. In truth, Carter has scant experience with children and he does tend to be a bit impatient and short with the kids who came along in the "Barbara package."

It gets even more difficult when the kids call their dad

or their grandparents every time they think Carter has done something wrong. After one of these calls, Bootsie or Mort gets on the phone with Barbara to rehash all the old recriminations about how foolish she was for leaving her "perfectly wonderful" first husband. If Carter gets wind of these conversations, it usually means that he and Barbara will have an ugly argument later. The parents have been told not to interfere, but so far, they aren't listening.

In general, the "rules" for parents and in-laws in a second—or third—marriage are the same as those for a first marriage. The most important principle is the commitment on the part of the couple to stand together against outside negative influence. Jesse and Richard and Carter and Barbara will continue to have difficulties unless they commit to standing together. It is important that they let those who are interfering know how they feel and make them aware of the limits they are setting. If all else fails, it may be necessary to distance themselves from parents and in-laws, at least temporarily. If a permanent distancing is needed, then that is what they must do.

He Wouldn't Keep His Father Quiet

Leona left Jeb after only two years of marriage. It was devastating because it was a second marriage for each, and they had vowed to make it work. Leona had thought they had a good chance for a happy life. After all, she and Jeb were mature, both in their forties, and their combined five children were well on their way to their own lives.

Unfortunately, Jeb's father took a dislike to Leona, whom he didn't meet until after the marriage. He called her a golddigger, which was ridiculous since Leona had money of her own, and Jeb had an average income. She and Jeb were restoring an old farmhouse, and as anyone who has ever embarked on such a project knows, this huge undertaking is not a project that is started one month and finished the next. Every time Hank came to visit, he complained that Leona was a "slow worker" and that Mona, Jeb's mother, who had died some years before, would have had the restoration done in no time at all. Of course, Mona wouldn't have had a career, which is the way it should be. Leona was one of those "aggressive, independent" types. (Leona was the administrator of a small charitable foundation.)

At first Leona laughed this off, confident that Jeb would finally have enough of this haranguing and tell Hank to be quiet. But it was not to be. Jeb would promise to say something to his dad. He promised many times. Every time Jeb approached his dad and started his "speech," Hank would start in on him: "You let your first marriage fail; you call yourself a consultant but you don't have a decent office or a secretary, and now you have this woman who bosses you around, and all she wants is your money anyway, and why don't you make her be your secretary. . . ." It was madness. Jeb knew it was crazy talk. But he never stepped in and stood up for himself, let alone Leona. Hank's hostility intimidated Jeb, and he backed down every time. What Jeb didn't understand was that Leona's respect for him was being whittled away. His inability to deal with his father or to seek help to examine why he was unable to do so finally wore down Leona's affection for Jeb. After two years, she left Jeb, who was heart-broken. Naturally, Hank thought it was all for the best. All he was concerned about was what price Jeb and Leona would get for their half-restored farmhouse. Leona vowed never to try marriage again, and when I saw her in counseling, she was rebuilding her life as a single woman.

This story is sad because it so clearly illustrates what happens when parents, and in this case, a particularly mean and irrational parent, are allowed to interfere in such a destructive manner. Sadly, no matter how old Jeb was, he did not have the maturity to draw a clear boundary with his father. Hank has been verbally abusive all his life, and until Jeb walks away from him, Hank has no reason to change.

The Most Fragile Tie

Children always have questions about their parents' divorce, and usually these questions are not adequately answered, which leaves them struggling to understand. Often, they imagine they are to blame. Even adult children will wonder if they were at least partly to blame. Along with these upsetting emotions, they may be conflicted about their loyalties to their parents and perhaps even to their grandparents. Some children are almost desperate for reassurance that they will still have both sets of grandparents in their lives.

This confusion over loyalties may intensify as they watch their parents become involved in new relationships. They may be jealous of the attention their parent gives to these "strangers." If the stranger has children, too, then it may be even harder for them to understand why their parent is involved with someone else's children. Already feeling abandoned, they now view themselves as even more left out. Many times I have seen children react to this situation silently and sadly. Their schoolwork and social lives may suffer, too. I have seen situations in which disobedience and rebellion become chronic problems, with some young people turning to drugs and alcohol as a means to escape their pain.

I cannot stress enough how critical the attention of loving, nonjudgmental grandparents can be at this time. All the adults in the family should understand that the emotional upheaval they are going through is never as great as that experienced by children, who may not be able to express their troubling, sad feelings.

Diversity Hits Home

Dave was not pleased when he saw his future daughter-in-law and step-grandchildren. He dragged his son, Kevin, into the kitchen and in a very loud "whisper" he said, "They're Vietnamese—why didn't you warn us that they're Vietnamese?" The twins, who were in their middle twenties, overheard this remark. Fortunately they heard Kevin respond, "Warn you? Warn you about what? I thought you were over your bigotry—it is the nineties after all. I wouldn't have subjected Mai and the kids to you if I'd known that you would react this way. Shape up, or we'll leave right now." Dave then realized that he had embarrassed himself, and he apologized to Kevin. Meanwhile, Mai and the twins were trying to carry on a pleasant conversation with Kevin's mother, Clare.

Kevin and Mai were married as planned, but Kevin limited his time with family, especially his father. Clare liked Mai and the twins, and they occasionally got together on their own, but Dave never did get over the discomfort of having Asian-American relatives. Kevin decided that his new family was more important than a relationship with his father. Frankly, Kevin was ashamed of his father's attitudes and deliberately created distance. He knew that an interracial marriage is difficult, even when both families are loving. He wasn't about to add additional tension. This was probably the best choice he could make.

Religion is another area that divides families, even in second and third marriages. I've seen blended families manage to practice two or more different religions, and when it works, it adds a positive dimension to family life. But when acceptance of differences is lacking, then sparks can fly.

I know that Dorian and Abel will never accept their new son-in-law's religion. They call it a cult, and to be fair, it does require an unusual amount of time and commitment.

From the outside, it could appear cultlike. So far, he's not attempted to recruit his stepchildren into his religion, but to Dorian and Abel, the threat is always there. Meanwhile, Dorian and Abel are trying their best to bring their son-in-law's children into their family circle. It isn't easy, but they are determined to help out any way they can.

Given the times we live in, diversity in families is to be expected. Dorian and Abel are making the best of a situation, and it is likely that some warmth will develop over time, at least with their new grandchildren. I admire their desire to be fair to all concerned.

Let's Be Fair!

Betty is engaged in a constant battle with her new in-laws and with her husband, and the arguments always seem to be about her children. Chris had told Betty that his parents were wonderful grandparents and her children would love to have them around. The idea of new grandparents for her children appealed to Betty. She considered Chris's family when she made her decision about marrying a man with kids of his own. Her own family lived too far away to have much of a relationship with her children, and her former in-laws were not particularly interested in the kids. Betty thought it would be good for the children and nice for her and Chris to have a place to drop the kids off once in a while so they could have a romantic evening at home. Betty's fantasy was far from the reality, however.

Yes, Chris's parents are generous and giving, but not to Betty's kids. All the kids are together for birthdays and holidays, and the so-called "blood" grandchildren receive a multitude of wonderful gifts. Betty's kids get a few things, but nothing in comparison with the bounty the other children receive. They show their favoritism in other hurtful ways, as well. They are always praising their own grandchildren but have little to say about Betty's kids. When Betty mentioned this and told her new in-laws that her children were hurt, they laughed it off and told her she was being silly. Her little ones were too young to understand!

Betty believed she had to put her foot down and set some rules. All gifts given to the children when they were all together were to be of equal number and value. Other gifts could be given at another time. And keep the one-sided praise within reason, please! Betty thought she was being fair, and it sounded good to me. The problem that finally brought them into counseling was that Chris didn't think all this was such a big deal, and he paid no attention when his parents broke the rules, which was often.

The loyalty one feels for one's children is strong. It is critical that Chris understand how strongly Betty feels about this situation and support her in the limits she has set. If Betty continues to feel that her children are being hurt by Chris's parents' unfair behavior, this marriage could be in trouble. One wonders, too, why Chris's parents are so insensitive and do not try to work with Betty and Chris on this issue.

Making the Effort

Second—or third or even fourth—marriages often mean an abundance of former relatives around and new relatives with whom relationships must be worked out. As you've seen, even planning a first wedding can become an emotionally draining experience. It isn't too surprising that second or third marriages can bring a complex tangle of relationships with them. I have heard the most amazing stories, not just from clients, but from my own friends and relatives. As I listened, I went along for a roller-coaster ride of emotions, from brokenhearted tears to hysterical laughter. Many family ties I heard described were warm and friendly; just as many were troubled and painful.

Sometimes the question becomes, "Is all this work worth it?" Most of the time I believe it is worth the effort to attempt to keep family relationships harmonious. It involves compromise and goodwill, two ingredients that blended families must have in generous proportions. Unfortunately, anger and jealousy stand in the way of the real work of blending families. Throughout this chapter, you've read about a variety of situations. It is sad, but most of the men and women you read about did not want to listen to the other side or make the compromises that would help repair a broken relationship. And that's too bad, because severed—or severely damaged—family ties are often painful, while good ones can enrich your life.

For divorced and remarried couples:

1. **Remember that divorce can be devastating for all parties,** even in a so-called amicable parting. Remarriage can be a difficult adjustment for all family members, including in-laws and children, even when the pair are madly in love. Family can be your greatest support. Turn to both families during these stressful times.

2. **Grandparents can be a great source of comfort and stability for troubled and sad children.** Invite loving, caring grandparents to help you.

3. **Do not forbid grandparents to see their grandchildren,** even if you are very angry at your mate or your in-law family. Your children should never be the victims of your anger.

4. **Do not allow your family and friends to speak ill of your former spouse or your former in-law family while your children are present.** If you do not wish to hear this negative talk, ask them to stop doing it. You are under no obligation to listen to anyone criticize your

children's other parent or a person with whom you shared a portion of your life.

5. **If you wish to maintain a cordial, even loving, relationship with your former in-law family, by all means do so.** This tie may be difficult to maintain and will inevitably change, but if you think it is worth the effort, go ahead and try.

6. **Do not insist that your children love their new family.** Allow them to remain loyal to the parent and family they have loved all their lives. Give them plenty of time for the new relationship to evolve.

For the parents:

1. **Recognize how painful divorce can be.** You may have experienced it yourself. Remarriage, as you may know, can be difficult, too. Freely offer your love and support to family members who are having a difficult time coping.

2. **Do not judge or criticize.** Above all else, withhold any comments or attitudes that smack of "I told you so." Brothers and sisters should heed this advice as well.

3. **Do not speak badly of any of the parties involved,** especially in front of the children. But even when you are alone with your adult child or sibling, refrain from playing the "blame game." Anger produces all kinds of accusations and recriminations. Try to steer clear of these judgmental discussions.

4. **If new children become part of your family, be as fair as possible.** Remember that children are easily hurt. Do not show favoritism.

5. **You do not have to love your new in-law child, but do give the relationship time before you make judgments.**

7 WHEN PARENTS GROW OLD

Before the wedding, when couples are talking about their future together, few if any think about the possibility that a parent may one day become dependent on them. In general, when people in their twenties or thirties fantasize about the future, they almost never say, "And then, one day, when your parents are old, and possibly sick, and maybe even need full-time care, they can move in with us!"

Many family issues may change as parents and in-laws age. Responsibilities shift, and problems between siblings and in-law siblings also may develop. This is a time when resentments build or old resentments and hurts surface. Sometimes just the strain of dealing with these problems takes its toll, and tempers flare.

Mamma Moves In

Don't talk to Lenore about family ties. She's had all the ties she can handle. "I absolutely cannot stand another minute with my mother living in my house," she said. "Doesn't she know that I'm a grown woman with teenage children?

Doesn't she know I've cooked thousands of meals and spent hundreds of hours cleaning and shopping without her telling me I'm doing it wrong? Why can't she mind her own business? I feel like she's choking me to death!"

This family tie is being strained to the breaking point. For years Lenore and Alberta had a fairly good relationship. They weren't extremely close, but they got on well with each other during the limited time they spent together. However, after Lenore's father died last year, everything changed. Lenore's brothers persuaded her to let their newly widowed—and very depressed—mother move in with her family. Now that Alberta is in Lenore's home, old issues are coming up. When Lenore was a teenager, she and her mother did not see eye to eye on much of anything. Between the natural strain of having a new person in the household and unresolved issues hanging in the air, the atmosphere is chilly. Lenore and Alberta are tiptoeing around each other, trying to avoid spending too much time together under this one roof.

To add to Lenore's problems, things are not going smoothly with her brothers. She has almost daily arguments with them and is angry that they are not doing their share. She resents that, somehow, she ended up being the sole caretaker of their mother. Now how did that happen? Even though she invited her mother to move in, she believes she was pressured to do so by her brothers. No wonder Lenore finds herself constantly tense over the frequent, hostile exchanges with her brothers and her mother. And, of course, she misses her privacy and longs for what used to be a calm, peaceful life—even with teenagers in the house.

Speaking of the teenagers, they are not happy either. The girls used to look forward to their grandmother's visits, but now they find her presence annoying, and they complain to their mother that their grandmother interferes and is "too nosy." As if that weren't enough, they don't like sharing their already cluttered bathroom with their grandmother. What a surprise! As it is, they have enough trouble sharing it with each other, and they fight over the hair dryer and the makeup mirror and the "shower schedule." Being adolescents, they resent giving up their precious "beauty-care" time, and now they have to make room for Grandma's medication bottles and other "junk," as they so tactfully put it.

How does Grandma feel about her new arrangement? This is very difficult for her. She is the one who has lost a lifelong mate, and she is the one who has had to adjust to a new home. She misses her husband terribly, and she also misses her quiet, uncluttered house. Alberta is very uncomfortable in the new environment, especially with all the commotion and endless activity that is typical when two teenagers are in the house. As a matter of fact, she finds the situation almost unbearable. And she knows she isn't really welcome.

Wow! It's easy to sympathize with all these "characters," isn't it? Everyone involved feels forced into this situation, except for the brothers, of course. Most people find their own surroundings and routines comfortable—and comforting. We need time to adjust to new family members in the household, and we would all need time to adjust to being the new family member. It is important that Lenore and Alberta understand that problems are bound to occur.

The Old Sabers Rattle

Lenore and Alberta must also understand that when the generations gather again under one roof, usually after many years of separation (at least in our culture), everyone is reminded of old battles that may have been underground for decades. For the most part, Lenore believes she was loved as a child, but she also has some bitter memories. Several issues, most of which originated in her young adulthood, left some emotional scars. Lenore buried these hurts, but the wounds are now re-opened and inflamed.

With some help, Lenore will probably be able to work through the old hurts, and even if another arrangement is made for Alberta, she and her mother will probably be able to reestablish a peaceful relationship. Overall, it may be good for the granddaughters to adjust and perhaps even be forced to be generous to their grandmother, who had always been very good to them. This situation can be far more difficult, if not impossible, for grown children who look back at a severely troubled childhood.

I have worked with adults who were victims of abusive parents. Some of these parents were verbally abusive; some were physically abusive, too. Yet the adult children often believe it is their duty to be caregivers, usually because no one else is available to step in. In these situations, the stress and anguish, plus the hostility toward the parents, are almost unimaginable. Nevertheless, I have seen families adjust.

What's to Think About? She'll Live with Us!

When an in-law child is forced to be the caregiver, it can often mean big trouble. Lenore, for example, had to adjust to a mother who was being critical and difficult. Suppose it had been an in-law parent who had moved in? Depending on the prior relationship, Lenore could have been even more unhappy about the situation.

I'll never forget lovable Tony. He's so easygoing. Everything rolls off his back. Sure, he says, we'll take care of Mama. "What's the big deal? Now that Mama can't live alone, she'll just move in with us. Just because you and Mama don't always see eye to eye doesn't mean you can't work it out. Did you ever hear about an Italian mother in a nursing home? Over my dead body! We Italians take care of our parents. There's no more to say; I'll move her in next week."

Of course, what Tony really means is that his wife, Jeannine, will take care of Mama. Tony grew up in a household, much like many homes, Italian or otherwise, where the women were the caregivers. Let's face it, no matter how drastically family arrangements and roles have changed, some families still look to the women to take care of an aging parent, should the need arise. At one time, many women accepted this role. They may not have liked it, but they accepted it. If a woman did not have her own career, then she was expected to take on whatever responsibility for her parents and her in-laws was necessary. Even if a woman has a job, she may find herself in a position in which her husband or her brothers expect her to quit in order to take care of the parent or in-law. I've had clients who sought counseling because the women involved resist this pressure and are often furious that the men in the family just assume they will take on this role. In fact, marriages have been known to break up over this issue.

Believe me, Tony's insistence that his mother not be "put away to die" has caused some serious strains in his relationship with Jeannine. Jeannine has a full-time job and a busy social life, and she is not willing to take on the responsibility of having an elderly person in the house. Tony is quick to assert that Jeannine would be willing to make sacrifices, such as giving up her job and her friends, if the discussion was about *her* mother moving in. This may or may not be true.

While Jeannine's situation shares some similarities with Lenore's, one big difference exists. As unhappy as Lenore has become, she made the choice. Her husband Chuck, knowing that he would not be responsible for any of the caregiving, left the decision to her. However, Jeannine doesn't have a similar choice. According to Tony, she must go along with his nonnegotiable decision. "It's what we do in our family," he says. He expects Jeannine to "obey," so to speak, in this matter. Say what? Nowadays, this attitude is what often brings many a marriage to the breaking point.

Whose Responsibility Is It?

The human life span has steadily increased, and the miracles of modern medicine have kept men and women alive beyond all past expectations. It shouldn't surprise us that caring for aging parents has evolved into a major concern for families. Many middle-age and older individuals find themselves in a very tough situation. They are working to provide for their upcoming retirement at the same time that they are concerned about their elderly parents. As a friend of mine says, "There are so many gray-haired people taking care of white-haired people."

Suitable housing arrangements may not become an issue for older people who choose to remain in their own homes and for those who have the means to pay a full-time caregiver, should that become necessary. Some people may be able to manage most household tasks but need assistance with shopping or cleaning. Retirement communities that have various housing arrangements, including assisted-living and a nursing-care center, are viable options for those who can afford them. Subsidized senior citizen housing is available in many cities and towns, but despite that, a good percentage of older people are living in near or actual poverty.

Financial problems are important, but equally significant are the situations in which older people require emotional support and comfort as they struggle to accept physical limitations or the loss of a mate. As parents turn to their children for help, the way they communicate is bound to change. In some cases, family ties may tighten, even where they have been quite loose before. Perhaps these ties can become too tight. Old resentments surface, and relationships between siblings may become strained. I have seen many more sisters become angry at brothers than the other way around. Again, this usually comes down to an assumption that the women in the family are more "equipped" to attend to whatever extra attention or caregiving is needed.

The key questions for families to consider, preferably before a crisis occurs, are:

* Is it the children's responsibility to care for aging parents?

* Is it a parent's responsibility to anticipate the possibility that extra care will be needed and make sure that enough money is available to cover all contingencies? (Obviously, in many families this expectation is unrealistic.)

* Do adult children have the right to refuse to take on this responsibility?

* Are in-law children required to be involved in caring for a spouse's family member?

* Are the children and in-law children selfish if they want no part of this caregiving and refuse to become involved?

* Who should make these decisions?

* Is one answer right?

Tony believes one answer is right: Jeannine should quit her job and take care of his mother. Jeannine doesn't agree; she wants to look for another answer. Lenore ended up with her mother because her siblings thought she was the most

167

capable of giving the care. Lenore's husband, Chuck, isn't pleased with the arrangement, either; and let's not forget that Alberta isn't happy. In fact, she is the person who has suffered the most significant losses, and it is no wonder that she is less than pleased with her new life.

Obviously, these situations require thoughtful consideration and open communication. Too often, decisions are made, and the individuals most affected by them fail to speak up. No wonder so many people end up unhappy. Alberta, for example, could have refused to have her children make decisions for her. She could have asked these grown children to help her find a retirement center or a subsidized-housing situation. But, before she had the opportunity, the adult sons jumped in and decided everything as if they knew what was best. But did they? Perhaps they didn't examine all the issues and options.

It isn't surprising that Lenore and Chuck started counseling a few months after Alberta moved in. Their stated reason for seeking this help was that they were criticizing and blaming each other for the tense atmosphere in their home. Finally, they agreed that it was too difficult to have Alberta with them; as it turned out, they weren't on opposing sides of this issue. It was this new understanding that allowed them to make joint decisions. Together, they presented Lenore's brothers with a new menu of options.

"Mom has some choices," Lenore said. "She can live in a senior citizen complex nearby, and all the children can visit. Or she can enter a retirement center that has long-term care as an option if she eventually needs it. We can all pitch in to help pay for it—she can't afford it on her own. Or Mom can rotate her time and spend four months living with each of us." It is interesting that the brothers dropped that last option and refused to give their mother that choice. They preferred the first option, which would cost them nothing. The reality was this: They thought it was perfectly fine for Lenore to take the responsibility for Alberta, but they were unwilling to share any of it themselves. At some point, family members must be held accountable for what they will or won't do for an aging parent.

Insistent at Your Own Risk

Inga and Jack are another couple who faced a difficult road as they struggled to resolve their family problems. Inga was a good-hearted daughter who insisted that her mother move into her home. Of course, it is Jack's home too, but since she is going to be doing the lion's share of the caregiving, Inga believed that Jack had no right to complain.

Now, this situation is different from Jeannine's. In that case, Tony was insisting on a change that would not affect his life very much because Jeannine was expected to do all the work. Although Jeannine was miserable, she went along. Tony had been overriding her decisions for her whole married life, so this didn't "feel" new.

By contrast, Jack refused to simply accept Inga's decision, even after the poor woman moved in. He made it abundantly clear that his mother-in-law, Tara, was not welcome. He continued to voice his complaints and didn't care if his mother-in-law heard him or not. Naturally, this rude behavior upset Inga, and it wasn't long before this three-person household was a picture of stress and strain. By the time Inga and Jack showed up in my office, they were headed for a divorce or, at the very least, an in-house estrangement. Were they willing to live unhappily together for the rest of their lives—or at least until Tara died?

This couple represented one of my most difficult cases. When they were in a therapy session, they agreed to compromise, but once they were home, their agreements went down the drain. They seemed incapable of coming up with lasting solutions. Jack didn't like having someone else in his home, so no compromise was good enough. Besides, he didn't particularly like Tara. Inga stubbornly refused to think about any other arrangement because she considered caring for her mother to be a sacred duty. Her attitude could be summed up as: "If Jack really loves me, he would see that hurting my mother hurts me." Jack's attitude was: "If she loved me, she wouldn't ask me to live the rest of my life in an intolerable situation, in a home where I do not have any privacy." So on and on it went. Neither was capable of seeing the other's side of the story.

Can a solution be reached when each partner has such strong feelings? Well, sometimes yes, sometimes no. I believe that Inga and Jack were unable to resolve this issue because it reflected other serious problems in their relationship. I also suspect that they left counseling, in spite of my suggestion to keep working on the problem, because I refused to take sides. Both probably expected me to see the "justness" of their cause! I wish I could report that ultimately this couple had a happy ending, but I never saw them again. For all I know, they still may be battling it out.

The Wicked Daughter-in-Law

Over the years, I have seen some adults who love their in-law parents and welcome them into their homes. They are willing to share the responsibility of caring for the older person—in or out of their home—because genuine goodwill exists, usually as a result of many years of effort in building a relationship. Unfortunately, this scenario is rare.

Betty was furious with Arthur because she thought he was spending far too much time taking care of Rose, his ever-demanding mother. Rose would call Arthur with a list of chores and errands and demand that he drop everything and come right away. Betty was angry with Arthur for "obeying" his mother's commands, but she was also angry with Meg, Arthur's sister. Unlike most women today, Betty is from the "old school." She believes it is a daughter's responsibility to take care of aging parents. Why couldn't Meg move closer to Rose? Or why couldn't Rose give up that big old house and get a small apartment that Meg could easily take care of? (Being from the old school was not going to backfire on Betty—her parents are both dead!)

Naturally, Meg, who considered herself a loving daughter, was outraged at this suggestion. Who was Betty to dictate what was best for Rose? Imagine asking Rose to leave her home and a neighborhood she loved. Again and again, Rose has said that she enjoys her house and garden too much to leave it. In addition, she has neighbors to whom she is close, including Ben, whom she calls her "sweetheart."

Everyone in the family was involved in the argument between Meg and Betty, who, if the truth were known, had never been friendly. Betty had become known as the mean, selfish daughter-in-law, and Arthur was the "wimp" who would not set his wife straight. Arthur was miserable as he tried unsuccessfully to make peace with his wife and the rest of the family. This family's ties were unraveling fast as all the relatives put in their two cents worth. The only person who remained untroubled was Rose. She continued to call on Arthur whenever she felt like it. She was either oblivious to all the controversy she was creating, or she knew about it but didn't care. Unfortunately, we tend to want to make one person the "bad guy" of the family, and Betty could do no right, according to the others!

Different Parents, Different Problems

Sometimes grown children are shocked when they find themselves forced to face issues around the care of their parents. They may never have given the idea much thought. Or they may have thought about it, but dismissed it as a dreary notion and not worth worrying about. Those who possess more wisdom have talked about it and perhaps even made agreements or plans in anticipation of the time when they may need to deal with these problems. In the best scenario, the parents and the grown children and their spouses have discussed potential future arrangements.

In general, I've found that most people rise to the occasion and pitch in with advice, time, and even money when elderly parents need assistance. However, some grown children turn away from taking any responsibility. It is easy to say that these people are selfish and uncaring. But sometimes, when we look more closely, the parents themselves are the reason why help is not forthcoming.

When Dependence Gets Out of Hand

Lil and Carl are very dependent on their children, Amelia and Pete, both of whom live nearby. Carl is eighty, and a few years ago he suffered a moderate stroke. He is able to live at home, and Lil does her best to take care of him. But she is seventy-nine herself, and her stamina isn't what it used to be. Naturally, she turns to her children for help. Who else would she turn to? She asks that Amelia and Pete take her shopping, write the checks for her bills, and take care of all the household maintenance. Lil also expects them to drive Carl to the doctor and to his twice-weekly physical therapy sessions.

Carl has firmly stated that he will not consider a nursing home, and Lil says it would be too lonely for her, even if he did agree to it. Carl and Lil assume that Amelia and Pete will make sure that they spend their remaining years living in a lifestyle that suits them. They haven't stopped to consider that fulfilling all their parents' needs has become a heavy burden for the two grown kids.

This brother and sister have talked to their friends and have asked for advice from people who face similar dilemmas. Much of the conversation revolves around the role reversal that is taking place. Two people who were once so dependent on parents now have parents very dependent on them. Amelia and Pete have noticed, however, that their friends talk about services they can hire and help that is available. Carl and Lil have never mentioned any of these alternatives.

Over the years I have helped many families get the help they need. For example, Carl and Lil are not poor. They can afford to hire a service to do some housework and cooking. Because neither can drive, they qualify for the Meals on Wheels program. In addition, transportation services are available that will take Carl to the doctor and to his physical therapy. And Lil is perfectly capable of taking a taxi to the bank or to the mall. In other words, much of the work that Amelia and Pete are asked to do could easily be done by paid workers.

In many communities, counseling is available to help parents and children air their feelings and reach decisions about when and how to use available services. Remember, too, that resources in many communities are offered free or on a sliding-scale basis for those of limited means.

When everyone is reasonable, and family communication is based on love and trust, the children can freely help the parents find resources if necessary, and presumably everyone is pleased. The problems start when the parents decide that "hired help" isn't good enough. Such was the case with Carl and Lil. "Meals on Wheels for us? Are you kidding? Why would we hire someone to vacuum the house, mow the lawn, and clean the bathrooms when we have two healthy children who can do it for us? Don't be ridiculous!"

To most reasonable people, this sounds unreasonable.

The questions could be asked another way: Why would you ask your children to do your housework and drive you around when they have families of their own to take care of and you can afford to pay for the services? But Lil and Carl said they were "mortified" to think that paid strangers would do what their children should be doing for free. "We did everything for you," they said, "and now you want to let strangers take care of us?"

Unfortunately, Amelia and Pete had to force the issue. They went through quite an ordeal as they listened to their parents vent their anger and feelings of rejection. But in order to reclaim their lives, they had to define some boundaries. The fact is, no matter how stubborn Lil and Carl are, their grown children have had it with ridiculous demands and are holding their ground. Eventually, they hope their parents will understand.

Here Comes the Manipulation, Not to Mention the Guilt

If Lil and Carl had given themselves a chance, they might have found that they enjoyed life more when they were not dependent on their children. If they were to take advantage of the opportunities offered, they could enjoy the new contacts they make and the new activities. I've known men and women who ended up enjoying their rides on the community bus or their shopping trips accompanied by aides—and other older people. Had they not refused to consider such an "outrageous" idea, Lil and Carl might have enjoyed gatherings at the community senior center. I've seen many older people thrive and gain a new zest for life when they avail themselves of services for seniors. One rather feisty man in his nineties told me that he likes his Meals on Wheels a hundred times better than the meals his daughter sometimes cooks!

Some seniors, however, have an aversion to using community services, those that are free to all citizens as well as those that are private and must be paid for. When they refuse these services because "the kids can do it," guilt inevitably becomes involved. While some grown children willingly take on some caretaking of their parents, some do it because they are afraid they would feel guilty if they didn't. But not really wanting the burden, they find themselves unhappy and feeling guilty that they can't have generous feelings all the time. What we are left with here is a no-win situation. Guilt drives the children to take on the job, and the guilt continues to hang around because they don't like the obligation. There must be a better way!

Unfortunately, Nelson's mother, Ruby, does not know the "better way." Once she told her son that if he didn't come over she would "lie down and die." Poor Nelson—he believed her. He also vividly remembers that as a child and an adolescent, he was afraid that his mother would die. She seemed to be always resting because she didn't feel well, and she went to the doctor often and had vague "conditions." Nelson learned to be quiet around her and not upset her because tension was bad for these conditions, whatever they were. Naturally, he suspected that she had serious illnesses that could kill her at any moment.

As an only child, Nelson learned to watch out for his mother, and since his father wasn't around much, he became her primary confidant and "assistant." After his father died, he did the household chores, cooked the meals, and waited on her while she stayed in bed, too ill to get up. Nelson finally married, at age forty-four, and everyone who knew him was amazed that he had married at all. This was a man who went home every day after work to take care of his mother. How did he meet someone?

A new woman, Robyn, was hired to work in Nelson's

department, and a quiet friendship developed into love and eventually ended in an engagement. Ruby was not pleased and proceeded to try to talk him out of marrying—what a ridiculous idea! Nelson's aunts and uncles were afraid that if Nelson didn't have the wedding soon, he would never do it, and he'd miss out on his chance for happiness.

The marriage got off to a shaky start: While still on his honeymoon, Ruby called Nelson. She was sick and frightened about being alone, and only Nelson could help. Robyn urged Nelson to call one of the relatives that had been so support-ive, but no, home they went. "It's the first time my mother has ever been alone," Nelson reasoned. "She will adjust in time, but it is too soon. We have to go home to her."

As any outsider would have known, the demands never diminished. Instead, they increased and intensified. Ruby was "about to die" almost every day. Robyn insisted on counseling. She began to wish she had insisted on counsel-ing before they married. Her own elderly parents had urged her to consider Nelson's history with his mother. Was she sure he could break away? Robyn wasn't certain he could, but she had not had much luck with men, and Nelson, for all his faults, was gentle, kind, and certainly steadfast and loyal. But the honeymoon "fiasco," as Robyn called it, made her very uneasy. Robyn knew all along that she would always be referred to as "that woman Nelson married." Still, she held her ground.

Nelson reluctantly agreed to counseling, but he had a difficult time with his guilt feelings when he said no to his mother about anything—and she was always asking for something. Robyn, however, became strong in her stance. "No more daily trips to his mother's house. She can afford to get someone to shop and clean for her. And another thing," Robyn said, "Ruby is eighty-four years old. If she is really so sickly, why isn't she dead yet?" That was a blunt, rhetorical question, and it at least prompted Nelson to consider the fact that his mother had manipulated him all his life. Robyn wasn't through, however. Her position was simple: "Nelson must choose. Either he sees his mother less often or he won't see me at all."

Well, the honeymoon really was over! Nelson promised Robyn that he would limit his time with Ruby and that he would stop jumping at her every command. He succeeded— for a while. Then he would begin to feel guilty, so he'd go to his mother's to do an earthshaking task like changing a lightbulb in a closet. Obviously, this couldn't wait, and the job had to be done around nine o'clock in the evening, of course. The old pattern started again. For eight years, this pattern continued. This couple stayed in counseling off and on for these years, and although Robyn hung in with Nelson, she took steps to create a life of her own. For example, when Nelson was off tending to his mother's shopping, Robyn was taking computer or language classes. She went to movies with friends and joined a book group. She even took a three-week trip to Europe with her sister and nieces one year and toured South America with a college friend the next. She also visited her own parents. One day, Robyn called to say that the counseling was over for good—sickly Ruby was dead at age ninety-two, and Robyn hoped the problem had died with her. We'll see. It is difficult to predict how Nelson will fare without concerns about his mother to occupy his days. Robyn and Nelson are ready to retire now, and she hopes he will be willing to travel with her. If he's not, she'll have to take that trek across Canada alone!

The Subtle Martyr

Some parents, Ruby, Carl, and Rose for example, made it very clear that they expect their children to be caregivers. But other parents may be more subtle in their demands.

Frances, age eighty-two, is a quiet, sweet woman who claims that the sixty years with her husband were blissful most of the time. Before he died last year, Leno proudly boasted that he had "the best wife in the world, a real gem who never raised her voice or complained about anything."

Naturally, Frances was devastated by the loss of her lifelong companion. She mourned deeply, but she vowed to make the best of it and move on. Because she and Leno had kept to themselves and had only a small group of friends and acquaintances, life now is lonely for Frances. Most of the time she stays home and knits, reads magazines, watches television, or works in her garden.

While admitting to loneliness at times, Frances remains the uncomplaining woman Leno was so proud of. When her children ask her how she is doing, her reply is usually, "Fine, I'm just fine." When they ask if she needs anything, her answer is, "I don't need a thing. Don't bother about me. I can manage. I don't want to be a burden. You have your own lives to lead."

Frances sees her sons and their wives a few times a month and her daughters-in-law usually call weekly. The grandchildren are busy, and they write or visit only occasionally. But, according to Frances, that's just fine. "I understand. Why would young people want to be around an old person like me? They have better things to do."

So why does this family feel so guilty? Let's listen in to what else Frances has to say:

"What did you have for dinner last night, Mom?" a daughter-in-law asks.

"Oh, I didn't like what was in the house so I didn't eat anything. Old people don't have much appetite anyway."

The children ask why she didn't go out to eat at one of the local restaurants. "Oh, you know, on weekends everyone is with their families," Frances says. "I don't like to sit alone."

"So," asks her son, "why didn't you call us? We could have come over—we could have all gone out."

Frances is adamant in her reply. "Oh, I know how busy you are. I would never want you to drop what you're doing to visit me! Anyway, you should get used to being without me. How much longer can an old lady live?"

And the children's reply, just naturally, is, "Oh Mom!"

If you have a person like Frances in your life, this type of discussion probably sounds familiar. Many friends and clients have told me that this kind of subtle "I-never-want-to-be-a-burden-or-interfere-or-bother-you-in-any-way" attitude is common. The accusations and the complaints are usually understood, however, loud and clear. The guilt trip is piled on.

Frances was obviously lonely at this time of her life. It was also obvious that she needed to be more involved with other people, which would mean trying some new activities and making new friends. Her children might alleviate her pain and loneliness if they spent more time with her. Rather than this undercurrent of guilt-provoking communication, an open and honest conversation is what is needed.

Say What You Mean? What an Odd Idea!

It is amazing how difficult it is for some individuals to communicate directly, and it is *indirect* communication that usually leads to big trouble. Indirect communication comes in many forms. Saying "I don't want you to drop what you're doing to help me" is an indirect way of saying "I need help." Or what about, "You don't want to go to that movie, do you?" Well, does this person want to see the movie or not? Asking a question in the negative form—you don't want (or need), do you?—is one of the most frustrating forms of indirect communication.

A persistent "negative" communicator once asked: "You

aren't going anywhere on Friday, are you?" Of course, this question left me wondering what she wanted or needed on Friday. The only way to make sense out of this kind of question is to say, "What is it you need or want on Friday night?" With this particular person, I had to force the issue every time!

The same technique of forcing directness may work with Frances. Her children may have to pose direct questions to her in order to find out what she really thinks. Instead of asking her how she is, they may have to say, "We will be going to the store on Tuesday night. Do you need any groceries from the Quik-and-Cheap this week?" Or "We're going out to dinner at Egg Roll Heaven on Saturday. If you're free, we hope you'll join us. We can pick you up." Or "Hi, Grandma—I'm home for the weekend. Can I come to see you on Saturday at two o'clock?" Her sons may need to say, "Do you have doctors' appointments scheduled next month?" If the answer is yes, they may need to say, "Are you driving yourself there?" or "We can arrange to go with you—it's no trouble."

All this may or may not help bring about better communication with Frances. However, it will help the children clarify what they can or cannot do for their mother and mother-in-law. Frankly, people who are known to be such wonderful, uncomplaining, nondemanding people are among the most difficult people to deal with because they are usually indirect, and they love to feel good about being so "nice." They may even brag (although they wouldn't call it that) to their friends that they make as few demands on their children as possible. Meanwhile, their children may be attempting to interpret what their parent *really* means, and they know they are being manipulated.

More women than men tend to be indirect communicators, probably because women in our culture (and in many others as well) are trained to hide their needs and not make demands, or even requests. Therefore, they have to find other ways to get what they want or need, so they take the indirect route. Martyrs are often indirect communicators, and their behavior is largely unconscious. In addition, they may not understand the effect of their communication style on others because they believe they are so easy to get along with.

Frances's children, in-law children, and grandchildren have a number of choices. For example, some may find that they are willing to take time to help Frances with various chores, visit her just to keep her company now and then, invite her to their homes, or ask her to go out to an event or for a meal. They can resist Frances's unconscious guilt-provoking behavior once they understand her and are clear about their own boundaries. Anyone who is feeling guilty about an aging in-law or parent needs to examine the situation to find out what is really going on. It is possible that Frances will always stay in her martyr role because she needs it. If that is the case, her family can simply learn to ignore it.

A Serious Development

Dee and Henry thought they were a contented couple, but that was before Dee's mother died. Joe, Dee's father, was always a lively, funny, and very active man, but now he has lost his zest for life. At first this seemed normal, but the situation is growing worse by the day. Day after day he sits at home and cries—nothing Dee does cheers him up or shakes him from this dreary "routine." It is Joe's routine that has Dee so worried. Every day Joe gets up late, eats some breakfast, and then sits in front of the television set until he falls asleep. Sometime in the afternoon, he gets up long enough to eat some lunch and then he heads for bed.

His old friends call, but he lets the answering machine pick up the calls, or when he does answer, he claims that he is just too tired to see anyone.

It hurts Dee to see her beloved dad suffer. She decided that she had to make every effort to pull him out of this depression. Because she couldn't get Joe to leave the house, she began to spend several nights a week with him. She also took to spending Sunday—all day—looking after her dad. Between her job and taking care of her dad, Dee was exhausted. Finally, she convinced him to come and stay in her home for a while.

Settled into his daughter's house, Joe slipped into the same routine of watching television and sleeping. Grieving or not, this was just too much for Henry to tolerate. Although Henry had not been pleased when Dee spent so much time at her father's house, he liked this intrusion into their home even less. Actually, he had never got along with Joe anyway, and he didn't want him around at all. Kindhearted Dee accused Henry of having a heart of stone. This couple began to see their contented marriage slip away.

In reality, Joe's move to Dee's house was not helping his depression. Joe's intense grief was no longer normal mourning; he had developed clinical depression, which required medical help. Dee finally took Joe to the doctor, who prescribed an antidepressant and suggested counseling. This doctor specialized in geriatrics, and he referred Joe to a counselor who would see Joe in his home. He also recommended a grief group for Joe and for Dee. With all the concerns Dee had with her father, she had had to ignore her own grief over losing her mother.

Dee's situation is quite common. She didn't want to abandon her father, nor should she, while he was in such a desperate state. But neither should she abandon her husband. This situation calls for great understanding first, and second, compromise and setting limits.

Torn between Demands and Desires

I expect that readers will have various reactions to this story. For example, some readers might wonder how Henry could be so selfish. Just when his wife needs support, he gets upset. Why couldn't he have waited a bit longer before he started showing his unhappiness? Dee doesn't need trouble with him now. It is true that in the best of all possible situations, Henry would have been at Dee's side, helping her with Joe and supporting her as she made decisions. He might have suggested that Henry stay with them temporarily. It isn't that simple, however. The two men have some history, dating back to Joe's opposition to Henry as a suitable man for his darling Dee. Back when Henry was still in his twenties and "finding himself," Joe thought he would be a bad provider. Henry's feelings were hurt, and the two men had always been wary of each other. Joe was proved wrong about Henry, but they never worked to repair their relationship. Dee and her mother had always been a buffer between the two men, whom they thought were too stubborn to be friends. No wonder Henry wasn't thrilled to have his father-in-law around.

Some readers might wonder why Dee was so intensely involved with her dad. As an only child, she had always been close to her parents, and her father was the typical doting dad. During her lunch hour at her office, Dee had checked in with her parents by phone regularly. As they had aged, Dee had helped them in many ways, even financially. Since Dee and Henry never had children, Dee was able to give her mother and father consistent attention. So when her father needed some help, she was glad to give it. How could she do otherwise?

Other readers might say that Henry should have swallowed his pride and supported Dee—no matter what had happened in the past. If he really loved his wife, they'd say, he should avoid putting her in a position where she feels torn. His selfish pride and demands are part of the problem.

Perhaps a bit of the responsibility can be assigned to Joe, who refused to listen to Dee when she saw his problem developing. He stubbornly refused help, which caused more problems in the long run.

It's unfortunate that Dee's situation is not unique. The particulars may differ, but many individuals end up feeling torn between two people or two sides of a family. And it probably comes as no surprise that women most often feel these divided loyalties as they struggle to make everyone "happy." Dee was trying to do right by her father, but not neglect her husband. Meanwhile, there is Henry, arms folded across his chest, saying, "You're spending *another* night with Joe? How nice." Later he says (in words or by implication), "Oh, Joe is moving into our home? Good old Joe—the guy who thought I was a jerk. How nice."

It is probably every wife's fantasy that Henry would say, "Look, you know that I've always resented your dad because of how he treated me. I don't much care for him—and he doesn't like me much either. But you have to do what you think is right. I'll help you as much as I can. We'll figure this out together." I have known men and women for whom this type of reassurance was as natural as breathing. These individuals are able to recognize petty jealous behavior and control the impulse to make demands on a person who is already feeling pulled in two directions. I have seen marriages break down when women find the demands and pressures too much and their husbands refuse to accept that maybe, just maybe, they are part of the problem.

What is probably called for in many situations involving aging parents is a generous spirit. If a couple or the parents can start with the desire to understand, help each other, and put the lid on resentments—at least temporarily—then compromise and limits are easier to reach. Some problems arise that are unpredictable, and therefore, impossible to prepare for.

However, before the wedding and after, before these problems begin, couples must talk, talk, talk. They need to discuss possible solutions to potential problems. I don't recommend that people worry and fret about things that may never happen, but I do recommend periodic soul-searching about these issues. Quite literally, we never know what could happen.

It's Just a Little Drink!

Marisa is puzzled by her mother's recent upbeat behavior. She doesn't understand her mother's good moods, because her dad, Max, died only three months ago. Since they were such a close couple, Marisa expected her mother, Cora, to fall apart. She was prepared to help her mother through what she assumed would be a difficult period. In fact, Cora came to stay with Marisa for a few weeks just after Max died, but she grew weary of sitting around her daughter's home, so one day she made arrangements to fly home. Marisa tried to convince her to stay a bit longer, but her mother insisted she was fine and would be happier in familiar surroundings.

After several weeks of nightly phone calls, Marisa has become suspicious of Cora's high-spirited, chipper moods—and she talks a mile a minute. Moreover, she never says anything about missing Max or feeling lonely. Marisa wonders how she could have recovered so quickly. As the weeks wear on, Marisa begins to notice that her mother says many things that do not make sense, and if she calls late in the evening, Cora slurs some of her words. Concerned and puzzled, Marisa told a friend about her mother's behavior. "It sounds like your mother could be drinking," the friend says.

Marisa is astonished, and like many people in her situation, she denies such a possibility. Drinking, indeed! No one in her family has ever had such a problem. (Well, maybe Uncle Artie, and Grandma Millie did carry a bottle of scotch with her on every trip she took.) But is it possible her friend is right?

Unfortunately, it is not only possible but probable that Cora is drinking. Statistics show that a significant number of elderly persons turn to alcohol as a cure for their loneliness. Like Cora, many drink at home alone. They may start by drinking in the evening, the hardest time of the day to be alone. Drinking alone is an obvious way to hide a developing addiction, which often begins with one glass of wine or one drink. As the sad mood lifts, a second or third drink seems to make things even better. Cora had been a very light social drinker, but since the alcohol eases her pain, then why not indulge? Who can it hurt?

Grown children should be aware of the dangers their parents face from depression or alcoholism, as well as from dependency on prescription drugs and addictive behaviors. If they suspect that a problem is developing, they are wise to take action. Mixing alcohol and some prescription drugs is often dangerous, and many older people take a combination of medications. In addition, heavy drinking can damage the brain and cause other physical damage very quickly in elderly people.

Marisa made plans to fly to Arizona to see her mother. She was wise to refuse to ignore the issue and pretend it would go away. Martin, Marisa's neighbor, had advised her to leave her mother alone. "Let her drink if it makes her feel better. She's old and depressed, and if a few drinks help her feel good, then leave her alone." Martin might not be so cavalier if one day Marisa tells him that her mother has died from a fall she took while drinking or broke her hip or forgot to take her medication and ended up in the hospital.

Any radical change in behavior is cause for concern. In some cases, drug interaction could be causing a problem, and it may be resolved easily. However, addictions do not just strike the young; they are a growing problem among our elderly population.

I'm Sorry, He Can't Live Here

Lloyd feels terrible about refusing to allow his father-in-law to move into his home. But after fifteen years of marriage to Brenda, he knows that her father's presence would be intolerable. You see, Bob has been an active alcoholic all his adult life. Throughout her childhood, Brenda witnessed some fairly ugly scenes between her parents. Lloyd was raised in a similar environment, and he and Brenda have worked hard to overcome the problems they brought into adulthood. Lloyd considers the life they have built together too valuable—too special—to risk by inviting Bob into it. Brenda's mother recently divorced Bob, and now he is playing on his daughter's sympathy. But Lloyd and Brenda have talked about the possibility that their respective parents—and a couple of addicted siblings, too—could come around one day and ask for help. He is reminding Brenda that they reached an agreement: They would not allow their own or their children's lives to be seriously disrupted by alcoholism and the behavior they find distasteful and destructive.

This was a very difficult situation for a family that already has overcome so much. They sought help from a counselor who specialized in addictions, and of course, Brenda quickly realized that she was vulnerable to her father's manipulation. He was trying to make her feel guilty, and he had succeeded. Fortunately, Lloyd, without resentment or unreasonable selfishness influencing him, stepped in, and a potentially serious problem was averted. Bob ended up in a studio apartment, and Brenda and Lloyd continued to limit their visits with him.

Pick, Pick, Pick

No matter what Paul does, he never seems to get it right. Paul has been a devoted son all his life, loving and attentive to his mother, Anita, and obedient to his father, Ike. Paul was the most caring of the two children in the family, and when he married, he took his father's suggestion to live close enough to visit Ike and Anita often. In fact, Paul and his wife, Mary, thought it might be fun to have parents so nearby. It was fun for many years, but now Ike and Anita are aging rapidly and becoming very demanding and critical. Mary and Paul were happy to step up their help, but no matter what they do, it's never enough. After being generous with their time and their money, they have had it.

Paul admits that Ike was always a difficult man, and he and his brother were expected to treat Ike as if he were the "king" of the palace. He had demanded and received complete obedience from everyone in the family, including his wife. Much as Paul loved his parents, he and his brother often talked about how good it would be when they were old enough to have homes of their own so they wouldn't have to live under the same roof with their critical and demanding dad. At age eighteen, both boys left for college and never returned to their childhood home for longer than a week or two during breaks.

So, why did Mary and Paul agree to live nearby? Paul's brother didn't fall into that trap. He lives a nice safe four states away. Well, Paul and Mary idealized a version of "family," which is not such an unusual thing to do. Paul saw himself as an adult, no longer a child who was subject to the whims of his dad. Mary had only her mother, who was far away in another country. To young people in love, the idea of a warm family a few blocks away fit a mutual fantasy.

Over the years, Paul and Mary have second-guessed themselves about their decision. At times they think it was a big mistake. "If we ever move again, let's move closer to my brother," Paul says. Ike and Anita have become so demanding and critical that Paul and Mary may be forced to move. Ike is critical of Anita, often leaving her in tears, and both parents find fault with almost everything Paul and Mary do. Now the younger couple feels the stress in their relationship.

One day, Mary saw a notice in the newspaper announcing a weekly meeting of individuals who serve as caregivers for the elderly. One meeting was all it took to convince them they needed the support they had found. They were relieved to know that other grown children faced similar problems. Talking about mutual problems has helped alleviate their stress and clarify some key ideas. First, they realized that no matter what they did for Paul's parents, particularly Ike, no thanks would ever be forthcoming. Given his past behavior, it wasn't likely that Ike was suddenly going to become generous and giving. Second, no matter how hard they tried, they would never please him, and they would never make Anita happy either.

With the encouragement and support of the group, Paul and Mary were able to ease up on themselves. They set limits on the time they spent with Ike and Anita, and they set limits on how many "hoops they would jump through" in their attempts to please these difficult people. They are much happier now—even though Ike never fails to tell them how ungrateful they are!

Don't Bother Me—I'm Busy with My New Life

It is wonderful to watch elderly parents go about their own business, becoming or remaining active, perhaps making new friends and developing new interests. Saul, however, may have carried his newfound energy too far, at least according to his children and their spouses.

Saul was eighty-six, and he certainly thought he was old and wise enough to run his own affairs, and since he figured he had only a few years left, he wanted to make the most of them. That sounded good to the kids, but they were very surprised when he announced that he was going to China. These grown children—not so young themselves—tried to talk him out of it. He'd never expressed interest in "exotic" travel before, and besides, he'd be far away from his own doctors. Saul went anyway and had a great time.

Saul's second trip was to Las Vegas. Saul loved the place, said it made him feel young again, and besides the great food and the shows, he discovered gambling. What fun! Those killjoy kids didn't like this new development, but a few weeks later, Saul was off again. When he came home he called the kids and told them that he'd won a great prize.

The family was shocked when he introduced his "big win," Jolene, his new wife. Saul and Jolene had met in the casino, and the rest is history. The grown kids, the in-law children, and the grandchildren were quite naturally taken aback, but it would have been helpful if they'd been able to see a bright side. As Saul says, he doesn't have too many years left, so why not have a companion who makes him happy? End of story? Not quite.

Saul's children and their spouses are now focused on "what to do about Dad's outrageous behavior." They now assume that it is up to them to make decisions for an old and "foolish" man. One son wants to have Saul declared legally incompetent. That way, he will need permission to spend his money. Arlene, one of the daughters, thinks that is a terrible idea, and besides, Saul is so sharp no doctor would declare him mentally unfit. Another sister suggests "freezing out" Jolene. Just refuse to accept her as part of the family. They can tell Saul that he can't see the grand-children while he is living with "the tramp." That will surely make him divorce her!

I concede that these grown children have legitimate con-cerns about what may be irrational behavior, but they also sound pretty mean. Could they have another motive? Saul has lots of money that was "supposed" to come to them upon his death. Could they be worried that their father will spend all his money or, even worse, leave it to Jolene?

Elderly individuals often do make some radical changes, especially after losing a spouse. One of my favorite personal family stories is about my Aunt Ethyl, who was married for many years to Uncle Jay, a cheapskate of some renown. He had a policy that he wouldn't spend his money on anything he thought was too expensive, which included just about everything. Poor Aunt Ethyl. She just didn't have the courage to keep fighting him, and she did without many things she would have enjoyed. When Uncle Jay died and the estate was settled, it turned out that Ethyl had about *two million dollars!* Ethyl mourned about three weeks, and then she began having the time of her life. She can't seem to spend the money fast enough. She's doing everything she would have liked to do while Jay was alive.

Fortunately, the whole family was delighted for her, and another of my aunts, Ruth, who never liked Jay much in the first place, often says, "Good thing the tightfisted coot died now while Ethyl is in good enough shape to enjoy the money!"

Saul's children and their spouses should probably try to relax and enjoy his zest for life and try to be pleased that Jolene makes him happy. If they notice that Saul is signing over his house, his car, and all his assets to Jolene, they can talk with him about his long-term plans for his money. Their knee-jerk negativity toward Jolene has prevented them from learning anything about her. Who knows, perhaps she's the one with the fortune. Maybe she has two million dollars to spend on Saul! Above all else, children, no matter how young or old, should refrain from calling their parents' companions names like "tramp" or "gold digger."

No one can predict the future, and most parents genuinely do not want to become a "problem" for which their children must find solutions. Still, we live in a society where longevity is increasing and the number of children per family is dropping. Therefore, it is likely for any beaming bride and groom who walk down the aisle once, twice, or even three times, that a time will come in their lives when their parents and in-laws need assistance. To avoid untold stress and even heartache down the road, I urge you to communicate about these issues before they come up.

For the couple:

1. **When it is necessary to make decisions about care for elderly parents, consider what is best for the whole family.** While the elderly person's feelings must be honored, realize that he or she may not be pleased with the plan, at least at first. For example, a nursing home may truly be the best solution, but we can't always expect the elderly individual to agree. Even if he or she does agree, the parent may not like it.

2. **Involve elderly parents in your lives if possible, but even more important, encourage them to develop lives of their own.** It is sometimes difficult to adjust to the inevitable losses involved with aging, but activities geared to seniors are available. Encourage parents to become involved.

3. **If you find that your family cannot resolve some important problems, seek help. Individuals and agencies exist that specialize in problems of the elderly.** If the problem is causing difficulty in your marriage, seek couples counseling before misunderstandings result in anger and hurt feelings.

4. **If you and your parents or in-law parents do not have a positive history together, then limit the time you spend together.** You may have done this for years, and just because of a crisis, you need not believe that the unhappy family is suddenly going to become the Waltons.

5. **If your parents have not been accepting or kind to your spouse, do not expect him or her to welcome your parent into your home or happily become involved in their care.** Frankly, this may be a natural consequence of allowing parents to disrespect your life partner.

6. **Keep in mind that you and your partner may have different feelings about responsibilities to parents.** Respect

those differences and try to compromise. Remember, family life often calls for a generous and loving spirit.

7. **If your parents have not handled practical arrangements such as having a will, a living will, and arranging for medical and financial power of attorney, urge them to do so.** Remember, however, that your parents have the right to spend all their money, burn it, or leave it to anyone they choose.

8. **A problem with in-laws may really be** *a problem in your marital relationship.* You may need help to resolve your interpersonal issues before you can resolve the issues about your in-laws.

9. **The men in the family must realize that they have as much responsibility for the parents as the women in the family.** Brothers should not assume that their sisters will take on the largest share of taking care of parents; husbands should not assume that their wives will take care of *their* parents. I have seen marriages break up over this issue.

10. **If one of the siblings or in-law children agrees to take on full-time care or does the majority of the practical work for a parent, make sure that person is acknowledged and supported.** For example, in one family, three siblings agreed to give a sister and her husband a portion of their inheritance because their sister had put her own career on hold in order to look after their father. Although not legally bound to this arrangement, they did it because it was fair.

11. **Do not forget that your children are watching you.** They may model their own behavior based on what they see. They may need to make decisions for—or about—you one day!

For the parents:

1. **Make decisions based on what is best for the whole family.** No matter how well you get along with your children, it is usually best not to live with them.

2. **Stay independent for as long as you can, but be prepared for needing help one day.** Become involved with senior citizen groups and organizations that are familiar with the problems you may well face in the future —or may even be facing now. If you wish to live in a retirement facility with graduated care, make these arrangements before a crisis occurs.

3. **Don't expect your children to handle all your problems,** and avoid making them feel guilty because they can't. Look for help outside your family.

4. **Stay involved with your children and grandchildren, but do not make them your whole life.** Meet new people, travel with a group if you can, volunteer in community activities if you are able, and do everything you can to make your own life wonderful during your senior years.

5. **Discuss your plans with your children, seek legal advice if necessary, and make sure your estate is in order.**

6. **Make sure all your children and in-law children know your wishes and are aware of the arrangements you have made.** Unless some unusual reason exists, such as a serious estrangement, the children should be equally informed. Make sure they all know who has medical and financial power of attorney and are aware of the location of your living will and your will.

8 TIES BEYOND THE GRAVE

*M*arion and Harris were enjoying their after-dinner coffee in the home of their friends Risa and Doug. Marion admired the beautiful piece of pottery on the coffee table and picked it up to look at it more carefully. "Oh," she said, "I didn't know your daughter was such a talented artist."

Doug chuckled as he said, "No, no, Stephanie didn't make that. We bought it in Venice—paid a fortune for it, too—but I understand why you thought it was her work, since her name is printed on the bottom of it."

Still chuckling, Doug pulled Marion up from the sofa and led her to a painting hanging on the wall. "Look at this," he said. "Mimi's name is on this piece. In fact, every stick of furniture and almost every object that has any value in this house is labeled. That way, there won't be any question about who gets what when we die. We are counting on our system to prevent a lot of arguments after we're gone."

I was amused by this story when I heard it the first time, and in fact, after hearing different versions of it from many different people, I wondered if it was just a joke making the rounds. I've come to realize, however, that families are talking about these things and telling each other about the solutions they found to an age-old problem.

Material Moments

I don't like to admit it, but some ties in my own family have been strained, some beyond repair, as individuals fought over who should get this or that possession after a relative had died. Between my own experiences and those told to me by friends and clients, I have collected numerous examples of family upheavals that occur when parents and in-laws die. Some of the stories are almost impossible to believe. One woman told me that she has not spoken to her sister and vows never to see her again because this witchy sister took *the silver teapot*! In this case, the death of a parent resulted in the death of another family tie, too.

The Caregiver Takes All

Greta was alone for many years after Leo died, but she was able to stay in her own home. She and her husband had lived modestly but were surrounded by the possessions they loved. Greta often joked that many of her favorite things had little monetary value, but she liked that her house was cluttered with them anyway.

Greta's married son and daughter lived on the opposite coast, but another son, Dieter, and his wife, Rona, lived only a few miles away. Rona was a highly organized, no-nonsense type of person, and after Greta had a stroke and had to go to a hospital, Rona told Dieter that she would put things in order for her mother-in-law. The next day, she moved some things out. "If no one is living in the house, that's an invitation to burglars," she said. Dieter couldn't understand why anyone would want any of his mother's "stuff," but he didn't think it was worth arguing about.

Trouble began to brew when the siblings arrived to be with their sick mother. They were surprised to find so many of the things their mother treasured gone, and they didn't buy Rona's explanation. Jill, the eldest child, had a particularly bad feeling about "Rona's raid," but she chose to remain silent.

Greta had a second stroke in the hospital, and much to the family's surprise, she died without ever returning home. Good organizer that she was, Rona offered to take care of funeral plans, because the rest of family was disoriented by the suddenness of their mother's death. They eagerly accepted Rona's help. The will was read a few days after the funeral, and since no mention was made of the many odds and ends that Greta had, the siblings agreed to divide them up as equally as they could. They asked Rona to make a list of the things she had taken home, especially those things that could have some value. The siblings added that she could just keep the rest. Jill and her brother Hank were tired and sad, and they wanted this phase over with so they could go back home. Sounds easy, but simple things can become complicated when the death of a loved one is involved.

Rona had a plan of her own. "You know that I was the daughter-in-law who lived close to Mom," she said, "and I did her shopping, ran all her errands, and drove her to doctor appointments. And let's not forget that she came to lunch or dinner every Sunday—and I cooked all those meals. Mom always said I was the only one she could count on." From Rona's viewpoint, it was only fair that she be given first choice of some of Greta's personal things, which were most of the things she'd already taken home.

Well, if Rona had been a more likable person or had handled this division of the things differently, her plan might have been acceptable. But given all the other circumstances, Rona's suggestions didn't sit well. Rona's in-law siblings and their spouses had never liked her in the first place. Jill, in particular, had complained about Rona's cold, selfish manner. Now, Jill and Hank, along with their spouses, added cunning and conniving to their characterization of Rona. Dieter wasn't pleased with his wife's actions, but when his brother and sister attacked Rona, he quickly jumped to her defense.

Greta would have been greatly distressed had she known what was going on. She had been pleased that the family had got along so well, and the siblings had hidden any disputes from her so she wouldn't be upset. Greta would certainly have been sad that a bitter quarrel over her possessions could mean the end of the family ties she valued so much.

So what could Greta have done to prevent this development? It is ironic that some individuals who value family often leave so much to chance when they die. Some people with a large and loving family don't even have a will! Or even if they do, it divides financial assets and instructs the heirs to divide material possessions and dispose of everything else. This opens the way for one or more heir to step in and claim entitlement to certain things. I've seen people fight over microwave ovens and salad bowls! You can imagine what goes on when a piece of jewelry or a painting, valuable or not, is left without a designated owner. And let's not even think about the family picture albums!

Obviously, if Greta had made a list of her possessions with a designated heir or if she had labeled everything, a family problem would have been avoided. Rona would have received her share, and if she received more because she did help Greta out more than the others did, then family members would have had no grounds on which to object.

But Mamma Promised Me . . .

From the time she was a little girl, Elaine knew she would inherit her mother's engagement ring. Orleen, Elaine's mother, believed that as the eldest daughter, Elaine was entitled to the ring, and the other children would share the remaining jewelry. Too bad Orleen never wrote that down. She trusted that as long as she told the family what she wanted, they would happily go along. She never dreamed that her beloved children would disrespect her wishes. Besides, Orleen believed her children were far too close to fight over these things.

Like Greta, Orleen made a big mistake. I can't emphasize this enough. Her first mistake was not clarifying which people she included in the overall term "children." Elaine and her two sisters thought she meant them. They believed it was clear that the daughters should divide the jewelry, but brother Ken thought that certainly "children" included him, so he wanted his share. Brenda, Ken's wife, eagerly agreed. She was one of the children, too, since Orleen always used that term to include the in-law kids and the grandchildren. "After all," Brenda added, "Orleen always said I was like a daughter to her." Brenda has some other ideas and didn't hesitate to voice them. For example, the rest of the family was not happy when she said, "The ring that Elaine is getting is so valuable that she shouldn't get anything else."

Ken saw big trouble brewing, so he suggested what seemed to him like a terrific idea. "Hey girls," he said, "let's not argue about this. Let's just sell all the jewelry and divide the money!" Yikes. I hope he ducked when the flying objects were hurled his way.

These so-called girls were furious with Ken for his dumb idea, and soon other family members were coming up with solutions, which presented fine opportunities for everyone to take sides. So, in the coming weeks, relatives lined up, debated every side, argued each minute point, and accused each other of all manner of wrongdoing and faulty thinking. In no time, this family's ties had disintegrated.

The last I heard, Elaine had put all the jewelry into a vault, because she was the first person to get hold of it. Her sisters are angry because she won't divide it up until she is confident she is doing the "right" thing. Brenda and Ken aren't speaking to all three sisters because the women refuse to agree that Brenda should have any of it. Many of the other relatives are angry because they do not believe the jewelry is worth disrupting the whole family. So far, no one can wear the lovely jewelry. Who knows? It could sit in the vault forever.

Obviously, while they are alive, parents and in-laws have a profound impact on the lives of their children. What too many of us fail to consider is the impact we may have after we die. It's as if we reach out from the grave, so to speak, and help to unravel the family ties we may have worked so hard to put in place. In the starkest sense, wills and testaments—and the lack of them—are the final messages we send to our children.

Who Deserves What?

Marvin had made his fortune being shrewd and daring in the business world. To him, money was power—and he liked both. His children call him controlling and not the most likable man. Marvin always had great expectations for his children, and he was the major force in planning their childhood activities. He "allowed" his wife to make suggestions, but he made the final decisions about their education, the lessons they took, and other after-school activities. When they were grown, Marvin was fond of reminding them that he had given them the tools they needed to travel the road to success—and they had better start that journey!

One of Marvin's favorite lectures was about "marrying well." The right spouse, he claimed, could enhance their reputation and status. For the most part, his children traveled the road he'd paved, but one son did not marry up to his expectations. It took considerable courage for this young man to marry a woman his father held in low esteem, but he bravely went ahead.

Does it surprise you when I say that Marvin's in-law children were not particularly fond of him? In fact, they resented the control he exerted and complained constantly about his interfering ways. The daughter-in-law who was not welcome in the first place was feisty and openly argued with him.

One of Marvin's favorite topics of conversation was his will. He let his kids know that they could expect to inherit *millions*. "But," he warned, "you will inherit my money only if you deserve it." What he meant by "deserve" changed from day to day, and as I said, he interfered a lot. His "suggestions" were a regular event, and if the kids didn't adopt these suggestions, he began to threaten them. "You are making a mistake, and if you continue behaving this way, I'll have to think about taking you out of the will. I can't be leaving my money to such a foolish person." He also made suggestions to his children about "handling" their spouses. "Your wife spends too much money," Marvin would tactfully announce. "Better watch it. I'm not leaving my money behind for her to burn." He made other demands as well: "What do you mean you're busy? I need you here now. Don't expect to reap benefits from me if you can't give a little."

Marvin maintained this unhealthy grip until he died—at age ninety-six! It is easy to criticize Marvin's kids and suggest that they could have escaped his control by not being so eager to remain in his will. In the best of all possible situations, they could have ignored him and his threats. Remember, though, these children were raised with a heavy hand and were taught to obey without question. It was against their nature to rebel or disapprove—although each tried now and then.

When Marvin died, sighs of relief were heard all around. They didn't want to openly show it, but his children looked forward to doing some of the things they had always wanted to do, without fear of their constantly displeased father. At least that's what they thought their lives would be like.

It was not to be. Marvin had ensured that he would always have control, even from the cold ground. He stated that not one penny of his money would go to anyone who was not a blood relative. So much for the in-law children. And in order to ensure that the in-law kids never received any benefits from his assets, the money would be doled out in very small amounts throughout the lifetime of his children. When the kids died, the money would go to the grandchildren. Finally, the worst blow of all was that the small amounts his children would receive could be collected only after they accomplished specific goals he had set for them. So, it looked like Marvin's plan to rule from the grave had worked!

Marvin's story gives new meaning to the line from the old blues song, "God bless the child who's got his own." Why do the Marvins of the world continue to control so many lives? Because they can. Too many men and women let good years go to waste because they believe some pot of gold will be waiting for them. If I had counseled Marvin's children, I probably would have tried to help them explore ways to separate from his control and to be less concerned about what they would or would not inherit.

The Out-of-Favor Son-in-Law

Joan and Nick disliked Ira from the first day they met him. True, he did have some untrustworthy qualities. At age twenty-nine, he'd been divorced twice and had never held a job for more than a few months. Even worse, he had spent time in jail for selling drugs.

Mindy married Ira in spite of her parents' disapproval, and Nick and Joan tried to make the best of it. It was difficult, however, because Ira could "behave" for just so long, and then he was back to his old, irresponsible ways. Naturally, Mindy suffered, and Joan and Nick grew to despise their son-in-law. Even after two babies were born, Ira didn't settle down. Mindy ended up asking her parents for financial help to get out of some messes Ira created.

Nick and Joan were very concerned about what arrangements to make in their estate that would keep the money from falling into Ira's hands. They were sure Ira would take the money and leave Mindy. So, with that unpleasant scenario in mind, they wrote their will to bypass their daughter and son-in-law and leave all their assets to their grandchildren, who would receive the money directly at age thirty-five. Well, Nick and Joan died relatively young, and when Ira realized that he and Mindy received nothing, and even his children would not inherit for many years, he was furious. He had counted on the money to get out of debt—again. Mindy was more hurt than angry at her parents' surprising last wishes. She knew Ira wasn't trustworthy, but they needed the money. Mindy felt abandoned and suffered the rest of her life over her parents' decision. The message from these graves may have been wise in important ways, but it was emotionally devastating.

The Principles to Consider

It's easy to agree that we all have the right to decide who gets our money when we die. If we want to give it all to charity, that's our right. And it's unpleasant to think that grown children may look forward to receiving an inheritance from much-loved parents. So are the stories I've told true? Do children count on inheriting their parents' money? Without question, yes. It is a given that children expect to inherit whatever money and assets deceased parents have accumulated in their lifetime.

Should parents and children discuss terms of the will? If so, when? And should all children be treated equally? Are there general expectations and guidelines? What are the exceptions? It is true that for all the children who are lovingly and generously remembered in a parent's will, other children deserve little or nothing. Some children and in-law children have been greedy and selfish and are just waiting for the money to come their way. Others were not necessarily nasty or greedy, just absent. They may never have visited or called, but they are readily available when it comes time to read the will.

The best overall advice I can give to parents who are lucky enough to have some money left when they die is to think carefully about the message their will sends to their children. Of course, parents are not obligated to leave any or all of their money to the kids. Parents earned it, and they are entitled to enjoy life and spend it on themselves. A common saying is, "It is better to give with a warm heart than a cold hand." I think it is a good idea to share some of the extra dollars—if available, of course—with children while parents are still alive. My husband and I would rather host a family vacation now, when all our grown kids can be there together. This is not the same as "coddling" adult kids. We can afford to be a bit generous now, but our children are responsible for the needs of their own families.

I believe strongly that we all need to take responsibility for our own lives. If children—young and grown alike— learn that they can always get what they want from parents, they will expect that generosity to continue. If material things are easily available, children—even grown children—may never understand the value of working for something. This is basic common sense, of course. But we may need reminders. Be wise about how much and how often you give. Too much generosity can backfire.

A Common Lament—It's Not Fair

Everyone will tell you that Jenna and Howard are lovely people: kind, thoughtful, generous. They knew, however, that it was important for their children to feel proud of accomplishments, and they didn't want to spoil their kids. Unfortunately, they only partially succeeded in not giving the kids whatever they asked for. Their generous nature made saying no very difficult, if not impossible.

It was quite common for the three kids to call on Mom and Dad when they needed something. Sometimes these requests were practical; they needed clothes for the kids or furniture for the new house. About as often, though, the requests were more frivolous. By anyone's standards, a new luxury car or a vacation to the tropics is not a necessity. Myrna, the middle child, asked for money and material things more frequently than the other kids. Joe, Myrna's husband, made a decent living, but he had a very expensive hobby. He belonged to a club whose members collected antique automobiles. Joe fixed up the engines and made the cars run. Then he attended shows with the car and traded for a better one. Sometimes, though, Joe went overboard and bought a car without the money to pay for it. He would write a check and then later, when Myrna needed to pay a bill, the mortgage payment for example, she had to call her parents. She was often too embarrassed to explain the real reason they couldn't meet the payment.

Joe never thought about stopping this behavior. Why should he? The money always turned up somehow. Bobby,

Myrna's brother, had an idea this was going on. But instead of talking to Myrna or their parents about it, he decided that his parents should give him the same amount of money Myrna and her family received. His wife encouraged this greedy behavior because her hobby was collecting gold jewelry. So, Bobby thought, if my parents can indirectly pay for Joe's hobby, they can help me give my wife the things she wants.

It wasn't long before baby brother Dick caught on to this "scam." He accused his brother and sister, along with their spouses, of being selfish. He had quite a blowup as he told them how disgusting they were. This outrage was expressed just a couple of days after he had convinced his dad that he needed a few bucks for a new business venture. (The old one had just failed.)

The loving parents in this family were not doing their kids any favors, and the ties were badly strained. What happened here? Was it too much of a good thing? Perhaps money *is* the root of all evil. One of our biggest challenges as individuals and as families is to make peace with money. This family is going to be in big trouble when the parents die.

The Mighty, Almighty Dollar

In most societies one needs money to live. Money is truly meaningful only for what can be purchased with it. But for some individuals, money has other meanings, including power. The almighty dollar can indeed mean power. You have already seen examples of how power bought obedience and control, even from the grave.

To some people, being wealthy means being respected. Big spenders, or those who are quick to reveal the extent of their wealth, often want to be admired. Maybe they earned this money, maybe they didn't. It doesn't matter; they just want to be respected and admired for having a lot of money.

Money can also mean love to those who receive it. Renee was a young woman who thought her parents loved her brother more because they gave him more money. Kitty assumed her boyfriend must love her because he bought her expensive things. The other side of this is that the person giving the gifts and money expects to be loved for being generous.

Money also brings up powerful emotions, some of which are ugly. Greed and a desire for revenge are never pretty. Children who are waiting around for their parents to die so that they will get their hands on the money are not pleasant to be around. If you have ever met a person like this, you know how uncomfortable you are around them. Taken to the extreme, more than a few murders have been committed for financial gain.

I say this to make both children and parents aware of how powerful money is on the emotional level. If money represents love and power, two of the most intense emotions we can feel, then is it any wonder that money can shake loose family ties? I urge you to think about these issues as you manage your relationships and your money, including your estate and all your possessions.

Just Bury Me

Alan had been a much-loved father and grandfather, and after his wife died, he had lived with his daughter for a time. When his health deteriorated, he moved into a nursing home located near the family. Being away from his children and grandchildren gave him more time to miss his wife, so his last few years were lonely. At the end of his life, his primary pleasure came from family visits.

The family mourned Alan's death but took comfort that at last he was at peace. Thinking that it would help his children, Alan had planned for his eventual death years before. He left written instructions for a simple funeral and set aside money to pay for this modest event.

Julia, the youngest daughter, read the instructions with dismay. "No way," she announced, "are we burying Dad in a simple wooden casket. He deserves the best money can buy." Her brother-in-law, Todd, pointed out that her father had clearly requested an inexpensive wooden casket, but Julia insisted. "Of course he didn't want that," she said. "Just look at how he buried Mom in a bronze casket with elaborate scrollwork on it. It cost a fortune. Dad was just being considerate, and he didn't want us to spend that kind of money burying him. But if we all chip in, we'll have the extra money to do it up right." She then proceeded to tell Todd that since he wasn't really "family" anyway, it was none of his business.

Well, now that war was declared, Opal, Julia's sister, jumped in. "How dare you insult my husband? Of course he is part of this family. And of course we will do as our father asked. We could never disregard his wishes. And, by the way, if want to know who should not have a say here, it's you! You were never around once Dad moved to the nursing home. Why, you're more like an outsider than *my husband* could ever be."

Oh dear. This was too much for Richard, Julia's husband, who was offended by his sister-in-law's comments. "You know, Opal," he said, "you've always had the biggest mouth in the family. You have a lot of nerve talking about not being around. Where were you when Dad lived with us? If we saw you once a month, that was a lot."

What was going on? Before this, an outsider would have thought this was a friendly family, but now they were being vicious in their attacks on each other. It is possible that the sadness of Alan's death had made them stressed and edgy, which is a very common reaction. Perhaps the whole mess could be resolved when they come to their senses and are able to discuss their options in a reasonable manner. But it is also possible that secret feelings of jealousy and resentment were being expressed. If they aren't careful, they could become another family who soon will not be speaking.

In general, I haven't seen too many families argue over the type of funeral a loved one should have, especially when clear instructions are left. However, I have heard arguments over where a deceased parent should be buried. Because of the high divorce rate and a longer life span, many more second and even third marriages are taking place, which can mean more spouses to think about. The resulting problems can be bizarre.

Rest in Peace—If You Can

Helene didn't want to be buried next to her good-for-nothing first husband. He was a louse, she said, and she'd never rest in peace with him around. Her second husband, Patrick, told her not to worry. When the time came, he said, she'd be buried next to him—on the right. His first wife, Nora, whom he had loved almost as much as he loved Helene, had the left spot. Patrick bought the plots and Helene was not to give it another thought.

Patrick did die first, and on the day he was buried, Helene looked around to find her grave site. She spotted Nora's grave, but there didn't appear to be any more room. A distraught Helene asked Patrick's children what had happened. According to them, it was assumed that their father would be buried next to their mother and that Helene would naturally be buried in her own family plot.

Helene protested, but the kids said it was too late to change things around—not too late for Helene, though, to create a mighty family uproar when she began proceedings to have Patrick's grave moved to make room for her. A legal tangle resulted, and Helene's children became involved, some siding with their mother and some not. Once again, families were arguing about parent and in-law issues that extended beyond the grave.

Anita was yet another wife with a first and second husband. She was troubled thinking about her eventual burial site. She truly loved Abe, her first husband of sixteen years. But she loved Gene, her second husband, just as much and had been married to him many more years. So, to quote another song, Anita was "torn between two lovers." She was loyal to both husbands, and she had children from both marriages. Let's add an ingredient to make this even more complex. If she were buried in a Catholic cemetery, where Gene had his family plot, her Jewish children with Abe could be uncomfortable; perhaps the Catholic kids wouldn't like it if she were buried next to Abe. Anita was so conscientious about this that she worried that one or the other husband might feel abandoned!

Anita went back and forth, making a decision, feeling guilty, and changing her mind again. So when she died, she still hadn't finalized her plans, and the kids had to make the decision. What a battle! Her kids with Abe wanted her with him, and her kids with Gene wanted their father to have her nearby. Gene was her last husband, after all. I lost track of this family, and I don't know how it turned out. I hope that Anita is resting in peace, somewhere!

It is true that some people would not understand any of these concerns. They do not believe that the physical body matters, and therefore, where it is buried is unimportant. In addition, many people believe that cremation is the one sure way to avoid all this conflict—not to mention burial expenses. But think again.

Garth wanted his ashes scattered over the ocean. "The sea has been more faithful than any woman I ever lived with," he said. He had lived with a number of women and had several kids. Agnes, one of his daughters, said that her father would be damned to hell if his wishes were followed. Cremation was against her religion. Martha, another daughter, agreed with her, although for different reasons. She wanted a place to visit her dad, and the ocean wouldn't do. Saul, one of Garth's sons, had an interesting opinion. He thought the sea was an appropriate place for a wanderer and a lot cheaper than buying a casket. Another son, Jack, said he was too busy to be bothered, and he didn't care anyway. The women in Garth's life had their own ideas. One former wife, Keisha, said that they should dig a hole and drop him in. "He deserves to go straight to hell," she declared.

The death of a parent, particularly the only surviving parent, usually brings grown children and their spouses together to make funeral arrangements. The ensuing arguments can be over serious issues or petty nonsense. Either way, the spats are often reminiscent of past emotional eruptions. In some cases, the family always has been at odds on many issues.

I believe, however, that hidden feelings often surface. Sadness, remorse, and guilt are a normal part of mourning. For the living, this may be a time when rivalries and old hurts and injustices emerge. Disagreements about funeral arrangements do not always relate to practical problems, but often to the interpersonal issues that have been festering, sometimes for a lifetime.

If the family bonds have been positive, most controversial issues are worked out. But if problems existed all along, the death of a parent and the subsequent final arrangements may be the beginning of the death of family ties.

The Lingering Ties

Karl and Arlene came to my office for counseling after twenty-nine years of marriage. Both in their mid-fifties, they are an energetic and handsome couple who appear much younger. Karl is an accountant, and Arlene is an attorney, and both exude intelligence and confidence. After they sat down, Arlene joked that since she is the lawyer in the family, she would start building her case.

In essence, Arlene said that until now they had worked out their problems over the years together. But during the past few months, Karl seemed different. "He's cold and uncaring," Arlene said, "and he says mean things to me. Is he going through a midlife crisis? That would make sense, but I want my sweet-tempered husband back!"

Karl was patient while his wife talked, but when he jumped in, he was angry. "Arlene is quick to put the blame on me," he said, "but what about her? During all these years of marriage, she has put herself first. Well, maybe not ahead of our children, but you know what I mean. [I didn't.] I've hated her smug and selfish attitude. And I've been feeling down lately and need her support, but she's too busy. Busy with the kids and grandkids, her job, her friends. There is never enough time left for me or for anything I care about. When *my mother* died a few months ago, Arlene barely made it to the funeral."

"I was late," Arlene explained, "because the cat picked that day to become deathly ill, and I had to take him to the vet. And it wasn't *that* important for me to be exactly on time—as long as I made it there before we had to go to the cemetery."

213

Karl exploded. "What a weak excuse. You hated my mother. That's why you were late."

I knew immediately that this argument was about far more than being late for a funeral. Listening to their verbal exchanges supplied some good clues about at least a few of their problems. It was important to recognize that Karl had recently experienced a sad event of some significance. Just as important, Arlene seemed to think it was no big deal.

Karl was grieving. A few months had not been enough time to deal with the death of his only remaining parent. As I was later to learn, he was troubled by guilt about ignoring his mother, at least much of the time, during her last years. He was also angry at Arlene, who had never liked either of his parents and had never hesitated to say so— loudly and often. Now that both parents were gone, Karl looked back and blamed Arlene for her part in making it nearly impossible for him to be a more devoted son. At least that's how Karl was viewing it. He remembered all the times she had been too busy to help out or to visit.

This couple spent several months in counseling. Arlene had described a happy relationship and many good times over the years. However, important issues, such as Arlene's feelings about Karl's parents, had never been deeply examined, let alone resolved. For the most part, Karl had gone along with Arlene's "agenda" in order to keep the peace. Now, when it was too late to change his actions, Karl was rethinking his behavior and blaming Arlene for his lack of attention to his parents.

The Ties Go On and On

Unfortunately, Arlene and Karl's story is common. As children mourn the death of their parents, they may look back and experience regret, remorse, or guilt. Many wish that they had been more available to their parents or supportive during the years when illness or loneliness took a toll. If the in-law relationship was difficult, some men and women find themselves wondering if things could have been different. Some people, such as Karl, blame their spouses, believing that they played a role in ruining relationships with their parents.

As grown children mourn their parents' deaths, they may begin to ponder their own aging process, which already could be well under way! Morris, a friend who just lost his mother, said, "I didn't do right by my parents when they were alive, and Anna [Morris's wife] was always too busy to visit my folks in the nursing home. I wish she had kept the bond closer, but I could have gone myself. What will happen when I get old and sick? Why should my kids treat me any differently? There's nothing for me to do but live with my regrets and hope that my parents, wherever they are, will forgive me."

My suggestions for both parents and children are simple. To every extent possible, parents should make clear—in writing—what they want done with their belongings. From valuable jewelry to objects that seem like simple trinkets, all items should be accounted for. If you really want your grandmother's emerald ring to go to your eldest granddaughter, then I urge you to itemize it and make the list part of the papers that accompany your will. (And it goes without saying that you should have a will.)

If you have specific wishes about funeral, cremation, or burial arrangements, make sure those are in writing as well. Organizations, often connected to different religious bodies, can help you make cremation or burial plans. They even have forms that can be completed years in advance. Make your children and in-law children—and other relatives—aware of these plans and the documents that explain them. These plans are just as important, if not more so, if this is a second or third marriage and stepchildren are involved.

Some family members do not like to discuss wills and funerals because they find it morbid. Many people harbor superstitions about talking about wills and funerals. They may believe that talking about death can make it happen. But my advice is to force a discussion, if necessary. I've talked with many friends and clients who have expressed gratitude to their late parents for settling their affairs and making their last wishes known.

Children, including in-law children, should understand that a death brings up all kinds of feelings, some of which may be confusing and unresolved. It is not unusual for siblings to begin to snipe at each other, and in-law family members may be told, either politely or not so politely, that they aren't really "family." An "us-and-them" mentality can develop as the siblings either pull together and see to the arrangements or pull apart and choose sides in a dispute.

If your parents are willing to discuss their will and funeral plans, as well as the disposition of their material possessions, by all means do it. Discussing these matters is the sensible thing to do. You may prevent confusion and misunderstanding later on. Above all else, understand that you are responsible for the quality of the relationship you have with your parents. It is not your spouse's fault if you are inattentive and unconcerned about them. In addition, it is not your partner's responsibility to take over your job of maintaining this relationship. If you have regrets about the relationship, recognize that they are your regrets and no one else's.

If you are an in-law child in the family, expect to stand aside when some decisions are made. If you are asked for your opinion or preference, then by all means participate, but realize that old animosities may surface and ancient rivalries may erupt. Refrain from expressing your negative feelings about a sibling in-law during a time when emotions are running high.

Everyone involved should bear in mind that grief, including guilt and regret, can trigger anger and arguments. At times like these, many people are certain that they know exactly what the deceased individual would have wanted, but no sure way to know exists. As much as possible, try to maintain an attitude of generosity and affection. The grief will pass one day, but the relationships will, we hope, remain.

9 IS THERE EVER A TIME TO GIVE UP?

Remember Irene? She was the woman who was so upset over her son's marriage to Leslie that she hid in the ladies' room during the wedding ceremony. If you recall, she actually called Leslie's family and offered to bribe Leslie to get out of her son's life. Irene made Stan and Leslie miserable with her negative and sometimes even irrational behavior. Stan and Leslie, while bewildered and sad, tried to understand Irene's extreme reaction. With great patience, they talked with her and acknowledged her disappointment about not having grandchildren. The couple encouraged her to spend time with Leslie's kids, who were warm and friendly. They wanted to have a step-grandmother and made welcoming overtures toward Irene. Some family members suggested (more than once) that Irene become involved in a foster-grandparents program or seek other volunteer positions where she could work with infants and small children. Irene listened, but took no action.

Much to everyone's surprise, Irene accepted invitations to Stan and Leslie's home once they returned home from their honeymoon. Unfortunately, these were not friendly visits. Irene ignored the teens and was cold to Leslie. Stan and Leslie hoped this was just a phase that would pass, so they overlooked Irene's ridiculous behavior. Eventually, however, their patience wore out, and the last I heard they had decided to see a lot less of Irene.

If Stan and Leslie had come to see me before the wedding, I probably would have advised them to proceed just as they did. They tried everything they could to make it work—short of having a baby! Sometimes, however, solutions are not forthcoming. Stan and Leslie gave it their best try but finally were forced to admit that the ties might not be possible to save after all. Stan sees his father and other relatives, and often Leslie is with him during these visits. They are doing the best they can to cope with a situation that Irene created and will not give up.

Throughout this book, I offer suggestions about mending family ties that are on the verge of breaking. Let's look at some situations in which the individuals involved tried some practical suggestions.

Compromise, Compromise, Compromise

Joanne hated visiting her in-laws. She felt left out when her husband's family talked and laughed about people she didn't know and events she hadn't been present for. She cringed at their crude and off-color jokes and the cruel remarks they made about other people. Most of all, she resented the way they pried into her personal life. Apparently, no topic was considered off-limits. Joanne also noticed that if she resisted answering their personal questions or showed embarrassment, they took delight in pressing even harder.

For Jimmy's sake, she tried to fit in, but no matter how hard she tried, she could not connect with her husband's loud, boisterous—and very annoying—family. Joanne finally gave up trying to fit in and pleaded with Jimmy to stop the weekly visits. At first, Jimmy refused to even consider this as an option. "All the kids come home to visit on Sundays," he said. "I look forward to it, and besides, I'm not going to break *tradition*."

Joanne tried again, but eventually, after numerous scenes, buckets of tears, and ugly fights, Jimmy agreed to limit the visits to every other Sunday. Joanne agreed to join in the fun instead of pouting and acting bored. So far, so good. Joanne tried to at least pretend she was having a good time, but her forced smile and artificial laugh irritated her husband, who called her a phony. "I'm sacrificing every other Sunday with my family," he said, "so the least you can do is genuinely try to enjoy yourself—no more phony stuff."

When this couple came for counseling, they realized that many of the compromises they had agreed to make in their marriage weren't working. Their disagreements—and their anger—had escalated and become intolerable. When they first began to talk with me, Jimmy was eager to tell me about the compromises they had made, and he, of course, had given the most. "First, the compromise over visiting my folks failed," he said, "and now she's upset about the baseball games." It seems that during the first summer they were married they bought a satellite dish, which meant they could see all the baseball games throughout the country—and Canada! Joanne had agreed to the purchase, but she hadn't realized that she would essentially lose her husband to one baseball game after another every night. If Joanne wanted to watch television, Jimmy suggested that she settle down in the bedroom, where they had another television.

Joanne was not pleased with this arrangement. She wanted to be with her husband—they were newlyweds, after all, she reminded him. She nagged and nagged until they reached a compromise. Jimmy would watch baseball every other night, and on the other nights, they would watch programs Joanne chose. Unfortunately, this left Jimmy in a cranky mood every other evening, and he didn't hesitate to comment on how stupid her favorite shows were. The remote control was never far away either, and during every commercial he checked the baseball scores. Joanne ended up taking the "clicker" out of his hands in order to return to her program. This was not exactly wedded bliss! (It is true though, that the war of the "clickers" is a familiar game in many families, regardless of the length of the marriage.)

The months of resentment and anger had led each to conclude that their marriage must have been a mistake. Counseling was an attempt to at least try to understand each other's feelings. And they did need help sorting things out. Many sessions would be necessary to work on major issues, but in the meantime, they needed some compromises for their immediate problems.

For example, Jimmy could watch his beloved baseball games virtually every night without objection from Joanne, but he had to take turns using the television in the living room. In return for this major concession, he would cut their joint visits to his family to one Sunday a month. This was an unusual compromise, but they discussed it thoroughly and decided to give it a try. Of course, Jimmy could see his family at other times on his own. Since his family were big baseball fans, he arranged to watch games with them. This compromise worked because each was getting what he or she truly wanted.

I can hear many people thinking, "But Joanne still doesn't have Jimmy's company" or "Jimmy's family still has to put up with her disdainful attitude. What kind of compromise is that?" By definition, compromise means no longer clinging to rigid ideas, and while "sticking to one's guns" is admirable in many situations, it is not conducive to the spirit of compromise. The kind of compromise reached by Joanne and Jimmy would not be acceptable to everyone, but it is worth considering. Each was willing to forgo a strong desire.

Searching for compromise means a willingness to communicate, which is often easier said than done. Furthermore, compromise can occur only in an atmosphere in which a desire to understand each other's feelings and respect differences exist. Joanne and Jimmy were doing more than compromising over an in-law issue. In a sense, they were setting a tone for other issues in their marriage. For example, if Jimmy was really going to spend many months of the year watching baseball, then Joanne had a decision to make about how she would spend her evenings. Would she continue to stay home or would she see her friends or do volunteer work or take adult education classes? Joanne realized, as everyone eventually does, that marriage does not define one's whole life. Every person must develop as an individual and not count on a partner to meet all needs. After the initial compromises were made, counseling continued, and after several months, Jimmy and Joanne understood each other much better. This couple was able to implement a solution and did not have to give up.

Keep Talking

Rachel and Steve were allowing Rachel's mother to be the catalyst in their deteriorating relationship. A devoted grandmother, Lorraine visited Rachel and Steve often, and when she showed up, she'd say, "I just couldn't stay away another minute. I missed my darling grandkids." Because Lorraine pitched in and helped Rachel with the kids, these visits might have been welcome had they been restricted primarily to daytime hours. Unfortunately, Lorraine usually arrived late in the day and often stayed well past the kids' bedtime.

As much as Rachel appreciated her mother's help, she

readily admitted that Lorraine was not always pleasant company. When Steve complained about Lorraine's constant presence, she agreed with him. She even agreed to speak to her mother and set some limits on the timing of her visits.

Somehow, Rachel could never seem to find the right time to discuss these things with her mother. Oh, she gave it what Steve called "a timid try" but always backed off out of fear and concern that she'd hurt her mother's feelings. As Steve insisted and Rachel resisted, they ended up angry with each other. Finally, Steve said he'd take matters into his own hands and talk to his mother-in-law himself. Once Rachel understood that Steve was not kidding about this, she convinced him that it would soften the blow if they approached Lorraine together.

Not long after, Steve, Rachel, and Lorraine were relaxing in the den after the kids were in bed. The timing seemed as right as it would ever be, so Steve took the plunge. He told Lorraine that he very much enjoyed her company, but that he wanted more time alone with Rachel. He and Rachel had discussed this, he said, and they agreed about this. "Together," Steve said, "we've worked out a schedule of evenings when we prefer not to have company." Rachel quickly added that she welcomed her mother's visits during the day and had no desire to limit them.

Lorraine got huffy and defensive and accused the couple of being ungrateful. "I drop everything and baby-sit for you if you need me," she told Rachel. And she proceeded to recite a list of things she had done for them and the sacrifices she had made. Eventually, her anger turned to tears, and it took a little more time—along with more hugs and tears—before Lorraine said she understood.

If this family discussion had not taken place, Steve's resentment likely would have festered, and his relationship with Rachel—and Lorraine—would have suffered. Gathering the resolve and courage to talk about the problem made a big difference in this family. Lorraine eventually stopped brooding, although Rachel occasionally had to remind her that she was coming around too often and staying too late again. (In actuality, Lorraine needed a fuller life of her own. Rachel tried to talk to her mother about this, but Lorraine claimed that family was the only important thing in life—anyone's life! I add this because the obvious question here is why Lorraine would think it was appropriate to spend so many evenings with her daughter's family.)

Rules and Limits

You may not have given much thought to the extent you will be involved with your family or in-laws after marriage. Or you may have had some firm ideas about how these relationships would be once you were married. But if you and your partner have different ideas about the parent and married-child relationship, then you are likely to be surprised down the road. What is most surprising is that so few of us consider these issues before we marry. Once the problems surface, we decide we need to talk out the differences, but we usually mean that we are going to set our partner straight in some way.

We must be willing to talk with—not just at—our partner. If we aren't willing to do this, we are in no position to decide if we should try more compromises, resign ourselves to an unpleasant situation, or if we should, in the end, give up. Talking things over, making compromises, and if necessary, setting limits, may lead to a greater understanding of why you and your partner have such different expectations. These processes will remind you that you and your partner brought different standards, values, customs, and so forth from your unique backgrounds. Your values and customs are likely not any better, although they may seem superior to you. In the end, they are just different. Equally important, by talking things out, you will recognize that while your emotional baggage may be very different, you both have it!

These discussions are not about changing your views, but they are about learning to respect your partner's opinions. When differences are so great that compromise seems impossible, it may be time to seek an unbiased viewpoint. Counseling can be of critical help during these difficult times.

Sometimes individuals do not want to seek counseling because they believe it means that their marriage has "failed." Actually, couples who seek counseling often do so because their marriages are strong. It is a sign of strength to seek objective help for problems. Some men and women believe that counseling inevitably means delving into the past and churning up childhood hurts. Others think it means blaming everything on parents.

In truth, counseling may or may not mean extensive exploration of the past, and even if childhood circumstances are examined, it is not for the purpose of blaming parents but, rather, of gaining understanding about the many influences that shape us. And the time for setting limits and making rules on extended family matters comes only after you and your partner are in agreement about the way these family ties should be managed. Do not rush in with pronouncements about the way things *must* turn out.

It sounds as if the advice I'm offering applies only to couples, but it applies equally to the in-law and parent families. Parents and in-laws may need to talk things over, compromise, and set their own limits. We've seen that this is very important when it comes to issues such as baby-sitting or gifts or lending money. As both an in-law child and a parent and an in-law parent myself, I believe that sometimes the years of experience and wisdom the older generations bring can help alleviate many problems—Irene's example notwithstanding!

What Are Your Priorities?

I can't think about Helen without feeling sad. I worked with this woman for so many months, but we didn't accomplish the goals we had set together when she started counseling sessions. Helen had hoped to come to terms with a diffi-cult—and terrible—decision she had made. Unfortunately, she made a decision never to see her son again, and this choice is likely to keep her depressed until the day she dies.

Helen's rigid religion, which she follows to the letter, meant that she was unable to accept her daughter-in-law, who does not practice any religion. Helen had refused to see her son unless he gave up Alexis, a woman he deeply loved. I could understand that this mother had to be firm in her own beliefs, but I had trouble with her unwillingness to embrace her son in the life he had chosen, which is suc-cessful by our society's standards. But, as a therapist, I set aside my own beliefs and values and tried to help her.

In some of our sessions, we focused on examining Helen's priorities. Religion was first for Helen, and because of that, she had made a choice she must stick to—no matter how much pain she suffered. Next we shifted to coping with grief and loss. Knowing that her son would not be a part of her life, Helen was trying to move on and find some happiness without him. Unfortunately, she remained deeply depressed and eventually switched to a counselor whose religious beliefs were compatible with her own. We agreed that the new therapist would be more likely to help her reach the peace she longed for.

From my point of view, we have made progress in our society in that Helen's situation is no longer typical. In fact, it seems extreme. While many parents disapprove of their child's choice of a mate, perhaps even because of religion, few cut off the relationship with the child.

Helen's story points out that it is essential to evaluate our priorities. Is following a religion or holding onto an attitude more important than one's children? Most parents find ways to compromise and accept their children's choices, even if they fall short of approving of those choices. I urge you to evaluate what is most important to you. As you do, it may become more possible to accept what can't be changed and make the best of it, no matter how difficult that is.

Look at Yourself First

Let's assume that you have made extraordinary efforts to make the in-law relationship work. You have evaluated your priorities, talked things over, made compromises, and set limits, but all to no avail. This may be the time to look deeply into yourself. What is it about you that contributes to the problem?

Early in my counseling career, I discovered that clients come in to discuss an initial problem that is not really the problem at the root. The initial complaint usually masks a more serious, underlying situation. For example, a couple can be so focused on the in-laws as the source of their difficulties that they fail to look at their own personal and interpersonal issues. Ironically, these may be the very issues that prevent satisfactory in-law relationships, and they may have little or nothing to do with the specific in-laws. If individuals and couples are willing to work out their own problems, they may have greater success in handling difficult in-laws.

Let's look at some problems in which personal and interpersonal issues contributed to or even caused problems with in-laws.

Who's in Control Here?

Vera doesn't like her in-laws much, but she can't tell you why. It doesn't matter to Josh. He just says, "Too bad, they're my parents, and we're going to see a lot of them." Their conflict plays itself out in ludicrous ways. Josh invites his parents over, and Vera calls them and cancels. Josh calls them back, reinvites them, and when they arrive, the atmosphere is strained and chilly.

After a few of these visits, Vera suggests a compromise. She asks Josh to plan fewer visits, but they can be of longer duration. Josh does not accept this plan. As far as he's concerned, his parents can come as often and stay as long as they wish. He adds that he isn't fond of Vera's parents, but he wouldn't dream of limiting their visits. His stance isn't tested because Vera's parents have very busy lives and barely find time to visit at all.

This argument has been going on for ten years. Vera is now firmly entrenched in her belief that Josh is a mamma's boy. Josh thinks his wife is mean as well as stubborn. He also thinks that Vera uses the issue with his parents as bait to provoke him. Understandably, Josh's parents sense they are not entirely welcome, and they add their complaints to Josh's dilemma. Meanwhile, they continue to visit.

Counseling sessions are sometimes filled with angry accusations and hostile exchanges. Sometimes I think that Josh and Vera actually hate each other. Getting past this initial period of casting mutual blame took some work, and then we discovered that (of course) more contributed to this problem than just some in-law visits. Their inability to compromise symbolizes other harmful dynamics in their relationship. What are the real issues?

In Josh's household, his father made all the rules, and his mother "obeyed" whether she liked it or not. When Vera refuses to follow his wishes, Josh views it as a personal attack on his masculinity and proof of Vera's rejection of him in his rightful (to him) role as "head of the family." It is true that "thoroughly modern Vera" believes that "obey" is an antiquated, if not a dirty, word in the context of marriage. It threatens her independence to go along with something she disagrees with. Consequently, not only does she dislike her in-laws, she resents being told "how it's going to be" when it comes to making decisions about their visits.

Vera and Josh have trouble agreeing on the basic definitions of roles. Josh doesn't think of himself as chauvinistic because he supports Vera's professional ambitions and does his share of the household work. But when it comes to the "bottom line," so to speak, underneath it all, Josh believes his decisions are the tiebreakers. He has final say. This annoys Vera to no end, of course. How could he believe such nonsense?

Eventually, we began to understand how this major difference influenced many of the issues on which Vera and Josh have trouble agreeing. They discovered, with surprise, that control is a critical issue for both and that feeling powerless results in their feeling unimportant or even unloved. (Although very common, this is often overlooked—it is hard to see in one's own relationship or in oneself.)

Most of us enter adulthood with basic assumptions about the roles of men and women. Even the words "husband" and "wife" carry powerful connotations, which is one reason that the word "partner" is preferred by many men and women. The word itself connotes equality. The beliefs we formed as children and bring to our marriages are not easily discarded, so it's no wonder it may take time for separate individuals to blend their ideas and form a satisfying relationship. Josh and Vera are in the midst of their struggle to work toward compromise without threatening their self-concepts. If they can do this, their in-law problem will likely be much easier to resolve.

Dependence—Independence

Randi couldn't get through a day without talking with her mother. Sometimes she spoke to her two or three times a day. She turned to Mom for help or at least comfort if she was troubled by a situation at work or by a difficult decision facing her. How nice that Randi and her mother have such a warm and close relationship. But Milt, Randi's husband, was not so happy about it. "Is it so unreasonable," he asks, "to expect Randi to turn to me when she needs help or is troubled? Isn't marriage about being close friends and leaning on each other, not to mention sharing our deepest feelings?"

In the beginning, Milt was quite fond of Rose, his mother-in-law, but as he and Randi argued about her dependency on her mother, he projected much of his anger onto Rose. He accused her of not being able to let go of her daughter, and before long, he had little use for Rose. He avoided her, and worse still, he was unpleasant to her when he did see her.

Adults are lucky if they are close to one or both parents, but a mature relationship does not include an excessive dependency. Randi never thought about why she had the need to see her mother so much or talk to her every day—it seemed perfectly normal to her. She was so used to turning to her mother that she thought it would always be that way, and besides, she saw no reason to change. It was a long time before Randi understood that while friendship with her mother was a good thing, depending on her mother for support and approval of everything she did was an indication that she hadn't fully grown up. As a child, Randi had been strongly encouraged to take her parents' advice about everything. Making her own choices about most things was not even allowed. Her home was a loving one, but it offered little room for learning to stand on her own.

Many adults remain dependent on their parents, but for reasons quite different from Randi's. No two parents are the same. Some are wonderful, some adequate, and some are just plain bad. Some fall in between. Indifferent parents don't want or care to make time to offer support—they just don't think about it.

Unfortunately, parents who are very critical or negative or those who neglect their children or even abuse them often raise children who are emotionally damaged and needy adults. These grown children often still yearn for the love that was denied them, and they don't give up trying to capture their parents' love or attention. They spent their young lives this way, and as adults, they can't stop this pattern; sometimes they don't even know that they have the option to stop yearning for love that is not going to be forthcoming, a particularly destructive form of dependency.

Therapy is almost always called for in situations of extreme emotional neediness. Just as Randi was trained to be dependent, so too are other children trained to be dependent for different reasons. It is extremely important to recognize that problems labeled in-law problems may really have their root in these unresolved personal issues. Once each person in the couple begins working on these personal issues, they often find that interpersonal problems, including in-law conflicts, are easier to resolve.

The Many Faces of Jealousy

Like dependency, jealousy comes in many forms, and it is often the underlying source of in-law problems. Jealousy results from the cycle of influence in childhood. From birth through most of childhood, parents are the most important influence, and then during the teen years, or even earlier for some, the peer group becomes more important. Parental influence shifts again during young adulthood, particularly when young people are focused on love relationships.

For the most part, parents look forward to the day their children gain independence. Most of the time they are pleased when their children fall in love. But, normal as it is for grown children to turn to "strangers" for love and support, it isn't surprising that this development brings with it some jealousy.

Unfortunately, some parents view this adult stage as a loss. They fear losing their child to another person, and this image can be quite painful. On the positive side, these fears are usually resolved in time. The mature among us note the uneasy feelings, but do not let them influence behavior. We rise to the occasion and try to make our new in-law child feel loved and welcome.

So many in-law troubles begin when those who can't bear to be replaced as the main attraction in their children's lives stir up conflict. They act out their jealous feelings, all the while justifying their behavior by criticizing, sulking, or complaining. Meanwhile, the in-law child, and perhaps their own child, is miserable.

Equally as often, the in-law child is jealous. Insecure adults or those with low self-esteem can sometimes be frightened by the intense feelings their chosen mate has for his or her family. Rather than seeing that this capacity to love will spill over to them, they are afraid that there isn't enough love left over for them. As victims of insecurity, they may even question their mate's loyalty. Some go so far as to demand that their mate make a choice—"It's me or *those* people." They may even like the in-laws, but they grow distrustful and begin to view them as troublesome or interfering.

Once again, the so-called in-law problem is not truly an in-law problem. These troubled and unhappy individuals need to face their own demons and work on their unresolved issues. If they do, the supposed in-law problem may go away, or at least diminish.

Let's not forget that jealousy is not limited to the parent-child relationship. Indeed, sisters, brothers, grandparents — all manner of relatives—can display jealous behavior. Remember the sisters who couldn't bear to lose their doting brother and created monumental problems for the poor bride-to-be? In my observation, jealousy is the *primary* reason for an in-law problem. For some people, it is very difficult when a loved one bonds closely to someone else, too. (These people obviously don't understand the words to the popular kids' song, "Love is something if you give it away, you always come back with more.")

Why Do I Feel So Guilty?

Following closely behind jealousy as the "great destroyer" of family relationships is our old nemesis guilt. Partners may have their own personal or interpersonal issues of guilt between them, and the situation becomes much more complex as they try to work out guilt issues within extended family relationships.

The last thing most of us expect is to be asked to choose between parents and a mate. However, as I've worked with couples with in-law problems, I have discovered how common that situation is!

One or both partners are consumed with guilt because they believe they are letting someone down. They can't please parents and their spouse, so they feel torn all the time. When a son or daughter is in the middle, trying to appease both parents and the spouse, someone gets hurt.

Patrick's mom expects her son and his family to visit almost every week as well as to celebrate all major holidays with her. Patrick's wife, Jenny, has refused. She does not want to—or intend to—spend every weekend and holiday with parents-in-law. She tries to explain to her husband that she has lived on her own for the last ten years, and she has grown accustomed to certain rituals. Sundays are for lounging around, reading the papers, perhaps having brunch or playing tennis with friends, and catching up on sleep. As for holidays, they represent vacation time. Jenny wants to fly off to the warm, sunny islands she loves. She expected her new husband to adapt to her lifestyle, at least in some ways. After all, they're adults, she thinks, and they can make their own choices.

Well, in truth, this marriage was not made in heaven to begin with. At forty-two, Jenny is fairly set in her ways, and she doesn't want to change. Jenny says that compromise is possible, but it doesn't appear to be true, unless it's on her terms, which means it isn't a compromise but an edict. This couple tried counseling, but Jenny wouldn't agree to many changes. Patrick thought about divorce, but he's decided that he loves his wife enough to stay with her, even though he knows she is selfish.

Patrick has made a clear choice. He has put his wife's happiness over his parents' wishes. Naturally, his parents are going to be hurt when he tells them he will see them only on an occasional Sunday and not at all during the winter holidays. It looks like his parents will be spending Christmas alone. Patrick acknowledges feeling guilty but says he'd feel worse living without Jenny. This couple is no longer in counseling, but I often think of them with a sense of failure. One always has to wonder about the future of a relationship that has no room for true compromise.

Patrick is likely to continue to feel guilty, and what will happen when his parents become ill? How will Patrick feel when they die? Jenny's rigid stance will have consequences for both down the road. How will she handle Patrick's guilt over ignoring his parents and essentially redefining his relationship with them? Obviously, Patrick's parents were making unreasonable demands. No parent is "entitled" to spend every Sunday or every holiday with their children. But this family group gave up without ever really trying to work things out.

Guilt can be directly provoked by parents when they say things like, "I'm alone here, so why don't you visit?" or "I need help" or, worse, "You owe me!" But some grown children feel guilty even when their parents are not provoking the guilt trip. The kids may know they haven't been the best sons and daughters, or perhaps they have made calling or visiting their parents a low priority. Other demands on their time just seem more important.

SOME adults believe that getting married will actually relieve residual guilt about neglecting parents. For example, Greg thinks it's up to his wife to plan the visits to his parents' house and to make the weekly phone calls. That might work in some cases, but Stella isn't interested in this job. She has her own family to deal with, and she doesn't think it's her job to tend to Greg's family obligations. Can you imagine all the possible variations on the in-law problem? And let's remember that, apparently, Greg and Stella didn't talk about this issue before they were married. If they had, Greg would have known that he had to find another way to keep up his family ties.

When the Solutions Fail

Okay, you and your in-laws do not get along, and you and your partner seem to argue about your families all the time. A simple difference of opinion can turn into an ugly argument and hurtful words fly. Talking things over doesn't work, and in fact, it sometimes makes things worse. You try to make compromises, but they don't work either. Counseling helped for a while, and you worked out some personal issues, but the old family stuff keeps surfacing. You think more and more about how much you dislike your in-law family—and on occasion you loathe your spouse. So, what do you do now?

CONVENTIONAL wisdom tells us that we should work out a family problem at all cost. And it is true that unresolved issues with the in-law family can portend much unhappiness in a marriage relationship. However, conventional solutions don't always work, and you may have to accept that the irritating or even painful situation can't be changed. This may be the time to consider an unconventional solution—*give up trying to resolve the problem.*

Over the years I've learned that not every issue can

be resolved, and at times the best we can do is accept that something is not going to change and then figure out how we will adjust to it. What do we do when we have accepted that there is nothing more we can do?

The Three-Thousand-Mile Solution

Karla and Richard have agreed to move far, far away from Richard's parents. After too many years of quarreling about in-laws, they have given up trying to resolve anything. Instead, they are running away from home. Richard's work enabled him to make the choice to leave. This couple agreed that moving away from this unpleasant situation seemed like the only chance they had of getting Richard's parents out of their day-to-day lives.

Two years after the move, they say it is the best decision they ever made. So much for the adage about not being able to escape problems by moving away. That's just what Karla and Richard did, and it worked. Karla and Richard no longer fight about their in-laws, although problems do crop up again when the parents make their yearly holiday visit. But, as Karla says, "I can handle difficult people once a year! After putting up with them every day, once a year is a piece of cake." This solution worked because Richard agreed that his parents are difficult. If he had spent years defending them, he would have resented the need to move away.

Moving away may sound like a radical step, but think of how many people distance themselves from their families without ever stating that the reason for accepting a job across the country, for example, offered the side benefit of being farther away from family demands. Such a move also presents an opportunity for young people to achieve the independence they need to function fully as adults and later as marriage partners. What I am saying is that determining a healthy and workable proximity to family may be more subtle than the openly stated decision Karla and Richard made. Distancing can also be done in degrees. Moving a couple of hours away may work just as well as moving across the country. Such a move may send a strong message to difficult families.

Couples can also let their families know that they will be reducing the time they spend together or even suspend all visits until such time that they can agree to work things out to everyone's satisfaction. Parents and others in the in-law family may be hurt, but that hurt can be weighed against the risks to the relationship posed by continuing a destructive relationship.

We Agree to Disagree

This solution is a bit unconventional because it requires that both parties—and perhaps the families, too—simply accept that they will continue to disagree. And then the most important step is to stop talking about it. Tammy and Lloyd have vowed to never again discuss Tammy's parents. Tammy will spend as much time as she chooses with her parents, and Lloyd will see them only occasionally. After years of verbal abuse, Lloyd has decided that he will not put himself in a position to be openly criticized again. He told Tammy and her parents that he is no longer willing to put up with their abuse, and he will not change his mind. Tammy is not happy about his decision, but she also understands that further discussion will result only in more arguments. They want to stay together, so they have agreed to disagree.

The Most Drastic Step of All

If conventional or unconventional solutions can't be agreed upon, then at some point, one must consider if the marriage is strong enough to sustain the disagreement. Can you live comfortably while still troubled by your partner's inability to make compromises about the parents you love? Are you able to withstand the pressure of your partner's unwillingness to understand your feelings and take your side? If you can't, you must think carefully about your choice of a lifelong mate.

Difficult as it may be to face, it is possible that your partner's background, attitudes, and values are really too different from your own. Or perhaps the person you love has personal issues that interfere with his or her ability to make a realistic compromise.

I am not advocating divorce in the face of an in-law problem. I suggest it as an option when all else has failed. Painful as this choice is, I have seen situations in which it truly was the only viable option.

Food for Thought

Before taking the drastic steps of either cutting off all ties with in-laws or seeking a divorce, ask yourself, and request that your partner also ask, the following questions:

* Have all the options been evaluated and given a fair chance?

* Have you tried counseling—perhaps more than once and with more than one therapist?

* Have you considered moving across the country or at least far enough away that time with the in-law family is automatically limited?

* If it is your family that is causing the trouble, have you talked with them and requested that they change their behavior or at least stop making demands? (It is amazing how often the partner resists confronting a parent.)

239

* Have you tried just putting up with the boring Sunday visits or laughing off the interfering remarks? Remember, not reacting to behavior often results in a shift. If one of two individuals will not play a game, the nature of the interaction automatically changes.

* Have you tried agreeing to disagree? Just stop talking about the problem. Each partner is free to make a choice to visit or not visit, interact or not interact. It sounds radical but it may work.

* If you consider divorce an option, have you thought about how things can change on their own? The way your in-laws relate to you can change over time. If a solution is not possible today, it may be possible later on.

* If you do choose divorce, have you thought long and hard about what life will be like without your partner? A fair warning here: A bad in-law situation can be far more tolerable than a painful divorce and life without your beloved partner.

Most problems do have a solution, but it is still best to avoid the problems in the first place whenever possible. In the next chapter, I'll offer some suggestions, based on my own experience, for developing harmonious in-law relationships.

10 SUMMING UP:
A Personal Perspective

O^{ne} of the reasons I became interested in the dynamics of in-law relationships is that I experienced these struggles in my own life. I do not need to go into great detail about these problems, and I want to protect my family's privacy just as I have protected the privacy of my clients and others in this book. Let me simply say that, like so many of the people you have read about in this book, I learned that jealousy and guilt were behind many of my family's conflicts. In some cases, my husband, Fred, and I had issues to work out with each other, and when we did, the in-law problems eased.

When Fred and I were dating and during the "honeymoon" period of our marriage, it didn't occur to me that differences in the way we were raised would be that important in the kind of relationship we created. But being young and idealistic, I didn't fully appreciate the potential problems ahead. For example, in Fred's family, the man was the boss, and the wife and children went along with what the husband said. In my family, I learned to do things on my own very early in life, and I didn't take orders from anyone. Naturally, Fred and I were both in for some surprises. Whereas Fred assumed that we would live more like his family, for me, the modern wave of shifting gender roles couldn't happen fast enough—new roles for women suited my personality just fine!

When Fred and I were first married, we lived far away from both sets of parents. He was in medical school in Chicago, and I taught school there. We went through financial struggles, and we still tell stories about trying to get our old car to start on cold January mornings, but for the most part, we were happy. Independent of the daily influence of either family, we were free to make our own way.

Later, when our first child was born and we were back in our home territory, Fred's parents offered us the first-floor apartment of their house, rent free. Since Fred had to complete his internship and residency, we accepted—we didn't think we could afford not to. Fred's mother, who had always pampered and spoiled her first son, was happy to have him nearby to pamper again. Not surprisingly, this family "togetherness" didn't go well much of the time. Jealousy and guilt began to interfere with family relationships, but I didn't understand that Fred and I were allowing the difficulties to develop. Instead, I blamed my in-laws.

Over the years, especially after we settled in our own home, the relationships improved, but they could have been better had I understood the dynamics of family and marriage relationships. If I had to do it over again, I probably would have sought some outside advice when the troubles first started. I would have known enough to look at my relationship with my husband, rather than blaming my in-laws. Eventually, when I studied counseling psychology, the insights I gained helped me understand that if we had communicated openly with his parents, we may have avoided many problems. In addition, Fred and I should have set limits based on joint decisions. We all could have compromised instead of digging our individual trenches and refusing to budge. As a result, we all denied ourselves happiness and taking pleasure in each other.

Learning from My Mistakes

The early years of my marriage are long behind me, and of course, they can't be changed. But long ago I vowed to learn from the mistakes I made and use the past as a guide. For example, after living through the errors my husband and my in-laws and I made, I vowed that those awful mother-in-law jokes would never apply to me.

While no relationship is perfect all the time, I am pleased that Fred and I have loving relationships with our three grown children and our two in-law children. We love and respect and value the time we spend with them and with our grandchildren. And I think they are fond of us, too.

As a way to review the key points in this book, I'll combine what I learned from my own experience as an in-law child and a parent with what I have learned as a family therapist.

Let the Kids Grow Up

Treat your grown children as the adults they are. This sounds obvious, but it isn't always easy to do. Sometimes we continue to think of the kids as kids—too young and inexperienced to make their own choices. As one parent of a married child said, "Of course I know she should solve her own problems. But it takes years of experience for people to know what is right for them, and I have been living for much longer than my daughter. She should listen to me."

Mind you, this married daughter had not even asked for advice!

Let's use this woman's opinion as an example of what not to do—unless we want to be called interfering parents and in-laws, of course. Sure, if we "wise older folks" are honest, we think we could help our children make better choices, but that isn't the point, is it? First, the kids may not care to hear what we have to say, preferring instead to live their own lives and make their own mistakes. Second, they will inevitably be resentful if we butt in. Or they could be the kind of grown children that will do anything just to disagree with their parents.

My advice? Give your opinion only if you are asked. Go ahead, hope that they will listen, and then back off, even if they make a choice that displeases you. Respect their right to make an independent decision, and hope it turns out for the best. If it doesn't, don't say, "I told you so." Just hope they learn from the mistake, and be there with your support.

Learn to Respect and Really Appreciate Differences

One of my daughter's best friends is a young man who came from India to study in the United States. Their friendship has become very dear to them, even though their backgrounds and cultures are so different that they hold many completely opposite opinions. They spend hours in friendly debate, yet they seem to understand and respect each other.

My point is that in today's society, our children are likely to have friends and acquaintances who come from diverse cultures and backgrounds. Today's colleges, and many corporations, too, resemble a United Nations assembly. Your children will work, study, and live with people from all over the world and from every corner of our own country. Your children may fall in love and marry a person whose background is radically different.

As we've seen, some people like diversity in the abstract, but not in the concrete. Parents find all kinds of things to object to in their children's choices of mates. Some are understandable, and some are ridiculous. When the potential in-law child comes from a different—and perhaps even unfamiliar—background, parents may say that the marriage will have too many strikes against it. Or they may say that the mate will just "not fit into the family." Instead of looking at differences as problems to be overcome, why not try to view them as opportunities to learn something new and to enrich your life?

If it isn't one thing it's another. I've heard people use age as another reason to disapprove. The chosen partner is too young or too old. Sometimes insignificant personality quirks seem monumental. "He's way too shy" or "She's so friendly it puts me off." One family didn't like the future son-in-law because he liked stock-car racing. Oh brother! Perhaps the dislike is based on no reason. Like Nora, who said, "I just plain don't like her—she seems funny." A reason isn't necessarily reasonable.

If you believe you must voice an opinion, do so in a non-judgmental and tactful way. If your opinion is rejected, remember that you *will* be the in-law parent of someone you don't approve of. So accept it anyway and respect the choice your child has made. No more negative remarks. Be the kind of parent who can love without reservation and supports the decisions your children make. And equally important, try to see the positive side. The child you love so much may be very happy because of the relationship he or she has chosen.

Butting Out

It is so easy to become involved in your grown children's disagreements. They may even turn to you for advice and ask for your opinions and support. The young couple may even air their arguments in your presence, which pulls you into their disputes. And, as a mature and sensible adult, you may even have a helpful solution that is on the tip of your tongue. Beware! This kind of in-law/parent involvement may spell trouble.

Give advice only when asked but, in general, discourage your children from involving you in their marital disputes. Remember that your advice could alienate one of the parties. Taking sides, especially against the in-law child, usually results in bad feelings. When the couple make up, they may remember—all too vividly—what you said. The one who felt unsupported may believe that your advice was biased against them. The memory of this sort of criticism may be lasting.

Stay out of an issue even if your initial warnings have been proved true. For example, your daughter tells you that her husband is selfish and immature. Didn't you use those very words? What a dandy time to jump in with "I told you so." What if you remind her that you knew all along he would be like this? In order to hurt him, she tells her husband what you said. The couple works out their problems, and what do you know, your son-in-law grows up a bit. Now your daughter is angry about what you said, and your son-in-law may forever consider you an enemy. The momentary satisfaction of being proved right just isn't worth the long-term anguish it can cause. Besides, in matters involving reservations about in-law children, always hope you'll be proved wrong.

This "back-off" rule applies to other family relationships, too. For example, your son does not get along well with his father-in-law and turns to you for advice. What should you do? You could offer some suggestions, but be sure not to say anything you wouldn't say to the father-in-law directly. Your advice could fuel the argument, and if your son tells his wife what you said, she could be angry with you. It's her father, after all. Remember, too, that your relationship with your son's in-laws could suffer.

All in all, when we examine the potential consequences, it is usually best to keep negative comments about other family members, especially in-law families, to yourself.

What Are the Visiting Hours around Here?

Naomi visits her grown children and grandchildren all day Sunday, every other week. In chatting with her old friend, Ellen, she says, "My son and his wife think I don't have a life of my own. They're complaining that I don't spend enough time with them." Ellen is surprised and says, "I see my kids for a couple of days a few times a year, and they think that's too much."

As you know, no general rules exist to cover visits with grown children and their families. We can rely only on common sense. For example, *always call before you visit*. Some individuals may love unexpected drop-ins, but I have never met such a person, and I don't know anyone who has. Even if you see your daughter-in-law's car in the driveway as you pass by, and you spot the kids through the picture window, resist the urge to "pop in." (You can always park down the street and call on the mobile phone.)

If you have a fairly decent relationship with your grown children and your in-law kids, then you probably feel comfortable calling and asking if you can visit. But if the answer is no, for whatever reason, can you accept that graciously? If it is appropriate, arrange for a visit at a time that does not interfere with your children's plans.

If you want to earn a reputation as a really great in-law,

wait for an invitation. Of course, you are much more free to invite your children to your home, but be sure that you can graciously accept a refusal and plan a visit for another time.

Do not make your children feel guilty if they do not want to see you every time you ask. They may have other plans or be too tired for company. They may just want to be alone. Typically, parents like to see more of their children and grandchildren than the other way around. This is a reality of life. If it puzzles you or hurts your feelings, keep it to yourself. Consider this part of the proverbial "human condition."

Keep your visits short. I gave that advice to one grandmother who said, "Of course. I stay only three weeks." This grandma visits only once a year and travels quite a way to get there. She observed, however, that after the first week everyone in the house was cranky. What "short" means is going to be different for each family. Set limits early on, before a "tradition" becomes established. Company that stays too long, even welcome company, can strain relationships.

The Holiday and Special Occasion Trap

Many couples have bitter arguments about holidays and special family days. This is a time that parents can do their kids a big favor. Do not demand that they spend these days with you. Be understanding; be generous. Ask the kids if they have holiday plans. If they say they are going to be with the "other" parents, tell them to have a great time. No matter how traditional it has become for your family to gather on certain days, remember that other families need to be considered. With the increase in blended families, some people have even more groups of relatives to think about. Some of these people may have their own traditions. Maybe you think your heart will break if you can't have your children with you on special days, but be fair. Most people come up with compromises, and no doubt one will work for you. Remember, too, that every person in your family may not celebrate the same holidays you do. You may have to work around religious traditions as well as cultural ones. If you're lucky, you may be asked to join in and have some new experiences.

Some families agree to alternate holiday celebrations on a yearly basis, which can work well if travel is involved. Or the kids agree to spend part of the holiday with both sets of parents, which may work if the families live close by. My own family worked out the holiday issue by alternating the holidays some of the time or by inviting everyone from both sides to celebrate in one place. Many of the celebrations have been at our house, which means a lot of extra work, but it beats being lonely for the kids on special occasions.

Sometimes the grown kids or the parents will decide to take advantage of holiday vacation packages and go out of town for the holidays. Resorts and other vacation spots are filled with families during holidays, and I'm beginning to see families who view these vacations as "holiday traditions." I can understand being disappointed if your children prefer a family vacation during your favorite holidays. Still, try to be understanding about this and handle your disappointment without making the kids feel guilty.

It is always wise to think about the consequences of "winning." Let's say your child and in-law decided to take their vacation time around the winter holidays and are planning a trip to some balmy island in the Caribbean. You tell them how appalled you are about their plans, and you talk on and on about how much everyone will miss them, and don't they want to see all the relatives? So, they give in (probably after having a huge fight about it), and your in-law child resents your power to change their plans. What exactly have you won?

Holidays are stressful and difficult for many families, even those whose relationships are harmonious. When relationships are strained in the first place, a holiday apart may be the best thing. No family needs a person who dictates how each holiday is supposed to be and expects everyone else to happily go along.

Generosity Rules

When my son got engaged, a good friend gave me this advice: "If you want to be a beloved in-law, keep your mouth shut and your pocketbook open." I laughed, and while I wasn't convinced that this was the only road to a loving relationship with in-law children, I was fairly sure it could help.

Most people respond positively to generosity. Many couples, especially those who are struggling to make ends meet, appreciate financial help. While cash is often the most welcome gift, other things besides money can relieve the burden of not having enough money. If a couple never eats out because they can't afford to, they might enjoy a meal, as your guest, in a nice restaurant. Maybe new coats for the grandkids would help out a lot. Perhaps grandparents can offer to pay for music or dancing lessons if money is tight. If the washing machine or dishwasher keeps breaking down, perhaps you can buy a new one as a gift.

I suggested this kind of giving to Gregory, a client who spent a lot of time complaining about his children and grandchildren. But he didn't like my suggestions. "Why should I give them anything" he asked. "I deserve respect and love just because I'm the father and grandfather. I shouldn't have to buy their love." Granted, he has a point, but I don't see it that way. If you enjoy giving to other people, then you are probably generous in spirit, as well as with material things. Working with Gregory confirmed that he was stingy in spirit, as well as with money.

I want to make it clear that you are never expected to give material things or money when you can't afford to or conversely, to give excessively even when you can afford it. In earlier chapters, I provided examples of situations in which generosity got out of hand or grandparents spent money they should have been using for their retirement or to enrich their own lives. An offer to baby-sit may be the most appreciated gift we can give parents of young children. I remember how tired and stressed I was when I had little ones underfoot. I would have loved an afternoon to myself. My grown children are happy when I offer to watch their kids—they hardly ever say no to that.

Gifts are great; extremes aren't. Just be careful not to give too much too often. If you do, the gifts are likely to go unappreciated or the gifts will be expected and may be-come more important than the visit. And nothing is worse than a gift that is attached to a string. If you ever find yourself even thinking, "I've given them so much, why can't they . . . ?" then rethink the motives for your generosity. Give generously of your love, your time, and material gifts if you can, but do it without expectations of something in return.

Accept, Accept, Accept

As we've seen, the in-law relationship can be fragile. It often takes mature reasoning and greater than normal understanding to make it work. Parents may not always like the things their grown children and in-law children say or do, and they may not like the idea that guidelines and rules exist about visits and gifts. Parents might not like it when their feelings aren't considered. But my advice is simple. When you believe your grown children are being unfair, give them the benefit of the doubt. Much as they may be wrong in your eyes, your criticism will not be welcome.

I believe it is especially important not to interfere during the first year of marriage, when a couple begins to sort out the many differences they have brought to their union. Be as tolerant as you can of the decisions they make. Be as warm, loving, generous, and uncomplaining as you can be, but never intrude. Who knows? You may be pleasantly surprised that your children and their spouses may want to see more of you than you want to see of them.

By the way, this advice holds true for your grown children who are still single. They probably do not want your interference either, and they are as entitled to their independence and privacy as are your married kids. Sometimes a single child can believe he or she is not as important as the new family, so make sure you respect their current status and choices.

Get on with It!

If a parent has spent a lifetime devoted to family and little else, he or she may very well feel lost when the children grow up and flee the nest. Such parents keep looking to the kids as their source of pleasure and happiness. But get over it. Individuals need a life as a whole person, not just a parent, in-law, or grandparent.

Funny how it works. Men and women who have full lives of their own and are looking forward to their own activities usually do not have the time or inclination to be interfering or demanding. They are too busy enriching their own lives to become a burden on others. If you find yourself facing an empty nest, then plan now to make new friends, learn new skills, travel, volunteer. Just start, do something—don't delay. Children should never be your whole life. It isn't good for you or for them.

Two Sides to the Story

As much as I am loath to admit it, at times I was probably the "daughter-in-law" from hell. It took years for me to understand that problems within my own marital relationship were often the reason that my husband and I could not resolve some of our in-law issues. When couples are having problems, it is much easier to point the finger elsewhere. I always had my in-laws to blame. But by blaming in this way, the problems Fred and I had either escalated or reinforced the difficulties with our in-laws.

Ultimately, Fred and I had to examine our relationship, and that is the advice I give to you. This is not to say that some in-laws aren't more difficult than others. But I do maintain that most in-law situations, no matter how difficult, are easier to work through if a couple can agree about how they will handle their own conflicts. This means examining what it is about their own relationship that prevents them from reaching agreement or compromise about these special family problems. I cannot emphasize this enough.

I also advise in-law children to give in-law parents the benefit of the doubt. Try to understand why they might be behaving a certain way. Are they having a hard time letting go of a child to whom they are deeply attached? Are they lonely and perhaps even clinically depressed? Do they feel unneeded and perhaps believe their usefulness is over? Are they concerned about their health and their own finances? Do they believe they will be left to cope entirely on their own—no matter what happens? Many women believe that their primary job in life was raising children and all other roles they play are superfluous. These women intrude because they don't know what else to do. Be as supportive and caring as possible, and perhaps this difficult time will pass.

One of the worst mistakes I made was not talking with my in-laws about the things that upset me. My mother-in-law was a warm, loving woman, and I think she would have responded to me if I had allowed her to see and understand more of what I was feeling.

In-law children are often afraid to speak up because they believe it will upset their spouses, and perhaps it will. But it is almost always better to have things out in the open. Better to have hurt feelings for a short time than have this hurt fester and explode down the road. I've seen years of resentment pour out in one big explosive fight because the issues were never talked about along the way.

Finally, if you can't find *anything* to like about in-laws who are nosy, intrusive, and obnoxious, remember this: They are your spouse's parents. Don't put your partner in the middle of these battles, and above all, do not try to get the man or woman you love to see just how awful these people are. Even if your mate is critical of his or her parents, be slow to agree with the criticism. Just listen. Recognize that grown children usually love their parents in spite of their faults. This capacity is precisely what allows your spouse to love you in spite of your shortcomings! Criticism of parents eventually takes an emotional toll.

The "Expert's" Last Advice

The opinions and suggestions presented in this book are based on my observations as a mother, daughter, daughter-in-law, and mother-in-law, as well as a marriage and family therapist. Does this mean I have all the answers? Absolutely not. I maintain in this book, as I did in my previous book, *When the Wrong Thing Is Right,* that your gut instinct usually leads to far better solutions to your problems than one provided by an authority or by conventional wisdom. I believe that encouraging men and women to follow their hearts is the best advice any expert can give.

My own personal experiences and years of working with

couples have revealed methods that may prevent problems with in-laws and resolve those that arise. I am sharing these observations with the hope that they will lead you to find solutions to problems that work for you and your family.

The ties that bind you to parents and in-laws do not have to strangle you. The bond you form can be flexible, comfortable—and comforting—nurturing, and even fun. When handled well, the in-law relationship can enrich your life and the lives of those you love.